DATE DUE

FRIEDRICH SCHILLER

WORLD DRAMATISTS

FRIEDRICH

CHILLER

CHARLES E. PASSAGE

WITH HALFTONE ILLUSTRATIONS

FREDERICK UNGAR PUBLISHING CO.

NEW YORK

CONTENTS

CHRONOLOGY

1759   Johann Christoph Friedrich Schiller is born (November 10) at Marbach-on-the-Neckar, in the Duchy of Württemberg, in southwestern Germany, the son of Lieutenant (later Captain) Johann Kaspar Schiller (1723–96) and of Elizabeth Dorothea Kodweiss (1732–1802), a Marbach innkeeper's daughter. His sisters are: Christophine (b. 1757), Louise (b. 1766), Christiane ("Nanette"; b. 1777).

1773–80   He is sent at age thirteen to the tuition-free ducal school (*Karlsschule*) at Solitude Palace, west of Stuttgart, to study law; transfers to medical studies (1775) when the ducal school is moved to Stuttgart and converted into a military academy; publishes first poem, *Evening*, in *The Swabian Magazine* (October, 1776); plays the title role in Goethe's *Clavigo* at a school performance of February 1780; writes the first draft of *The Robbers*, autumn of 1780. In December, 1780, Schiller completes his medical course and is appointed regimental surgeon to a grenadier regiment stationed in Stuttgart.

1781   Anonymously publishes *The Robbers* (June).

1782   *The Robbers* is premiered at Mannheim
        (January 13), with overwhelming success.
        Fiesco is planned (February). He is sen-
        tenced to two weeks of detention (June 28
        to July 12) for two absences without leave in
        order to go to Mannheim; the plan for *In-
        trigue and Love* is conceived during the de-
        tention; Schiller flees, under the alias of "Dr.
        Ritter," to Mannheim (September 22) and
        spends the next ten months as a fugitive.

1783   While living at the rural estate of Bauerbach
        (January–July) in central Germany, Schiller
        completes *Fiesco* and *Intrigue and Love* and
        begins *Don Carlos*; *Fiesco* is premiered in
        Bonn (July 20), with moderate success.
        From August to December, Schiller lives in
        Mannheim, where his expectations of a per-
        manent theater position fail to materialize.

1784   *Fiesco* is produced in Mannheim (January
        11), again with moderate success; in March,
        Intrigue and Love is published; that play has
        great success in Frankfurt-am-Main (April
        13) and in Mannheim (April 15). An oral
        reading of Act I of *Don Carlos* (the prose
        version) is done before Duke Charles Augus-
        tus of Weimar (December), for which the
        Duke bestows upon Schiller a pension and
        the title of Weimar Councillor.

1785   At the invitation of his new friend Körner,
        Schiller moves to Leipzig (May) and then to
        Dresden (October); he works on *Don Carlos*.

1786   Further work on *Don Carlos*.

1787   *Don Carlos* is completed as a blank-verse
        drama (April) and is published (June); it is
        given its premiere in Hamburg (August 29);
        through the summer and autumn Schiller

travels about the region of Thuringia and meets his future wife, Charlotte von Lengefeld, in the town of Rudolstadt.

1788   He corresponds with Charlotte; publishes *Letters about Don Carlos* (July and December). He is nominated (December) by Goethe for a professorship in history at the University of Jena, despite Goethe's seeming dislike of him.

1789   Schiller moves to Jena (May) and gives his first university lecture (May 26); his written proposal of marriage (August) is accepted by Charlotte. The marriage takes place February 22, 1790.

1791   Suffers from a serious lung infection (January) and serious recurrences of the illness (May).

1792   Suffers another recurrence of lung ailment (January). *Don Carlos* is first produced in Weimar (February 28); the *History of the Thirty Years' War* is completed.

1793   Writes the principal essays on aesthetics (May and thereafter)—*On Grace and Dignity, On the Sublime;* journeys with his wife to the region of Stuttgart (August and the rest of the year); their son, Karl Friedrich Ludwig is born September 14. Schiller's one-time enemy, Duke Charles Eugene, dies (October 24).

1794   His friendship with Goethe begins (July).

1795   Writes more aesthetic essays and a large number of poems.

1796   Schiller's sister "Nanette" dies (March 23), and then his father (September 7); a second son, Ernst Friedrich Wilhelm, is born (July 11).

1797   Works on *Wallenstein*: composes most of the famous ballads.

1798   *Wallenstein's Camp* is premiered (October 12) on the occasion of the opening of the new Weimar Theater building.

1799   *The Piccolomini* is premiered (January 30); *The Death of Wallenstein* is premiered (April 10). Schiller moves to Weimar (December 3); a daughter, Karoline Henriette Luise, is born (October 11).

1800   The *Macbeth* translation is premiered (May 14); *Mary Stuart* (June 14) is premiered; the *Wallenstein* trilogy is published in its final form (June).

1801   Completes *The Maid of Orleans* (April), which cannot be produced at Weimar until 1804; that play is premiered in Leipzig (September 11); translates and adapts Gozzi's *Turandot* (October–December).

1802   The *Turandot* version is premiered (January 30); Schiller's mother dies (April 29); Goethe's *Iphigenia in Tauris* is produced in Schiller's adaptation (May 15); Schiller is elevated to noble rank (November).

1803   *The Bride of Messina* is premiered (April 19); two French comedies by Picard, as translated by Schiller, are produced: *The Nephew as Uncle* (May 18) and *The Parasite* (October 12).

1804   *William Tell* is premiered (March 17); Prussian royalty arranges to have a lucrative theater position offered to Schiller (April), but he chooses to stay in Weimar; a second daughter is born, Emilie Henriette Luise (July 25); composes and presents the one-act *Homage to the Arts* (November) as part of the marriage festivities for the Weimar Duke Apparent, Charles Frederick, and Grand Duchess Marya Pavlovna of Russia; during an illness in December, Schiller translates Racine's *Phèdre*.

1805   The *Phèdre* translation is premiered (January 30); Schiller composes almost all of the *Demetrius* fragment (late February to early May); he last meets with Goethe; suffers acute lung inflammation (May 1), though work is continued on *Demetrius* up to May 5. Schiller dies in the early evening on May 9. He is buried in the local cemetery (May 12). Schiller's remains were transferred in December, 1827, to the ducal vault, where Charles Augustus was buried in 1828 and Goethe in 1832.

SCHILLER'S LIFE AND TIMES

Schiller is the greatest writer of serious drama between the death of Racine in 1699 and the emergence of Ibsen as a master of the European theater around 1880. This statement regards the intrinsic merit of Schiller's plays, their immense and extended popularity in performance, and their influence on subsequent dramatic and nondramatic writers.

Widely prevalent eighteenth-century notions had undermined the foundations of tragedy, as Shakespeare and Racine had conceived of tragedy. Optimistic trust in the perfectibility of man and of society had slackened the sinews that could shape *Macbeth* or *Britannicus*, and urbane skepticism had discredited myth as a vehicle for tragic expression. In urban centers, such as London and Paris, comedy throve, especially the comedy of manners, but verse tragedies about kings and princes had gone stale, and the prose plays about hapless commoners, such as *The London Merchant* of 1731 and Diderot's experiments with "tearful comedy" in the 1750s, were artistically immature. A new formula for serious drama was needed, and Schiller's plays around 1800 created that formula.

At the beginning of the eighteenth century Germany seemed an unlikely area for the development of a new dramatic form. While the upper and middle classes of society through almost all of central Europe spoke German, either natively or as a second language, they did so for utilitarian reasons, and the literary prestige of German was close to nil. The dramas of the previous century, by such writers as Gryphius and Lohenstein, had been forced hothouse flowers, bred for certain courts, and they had all withered by 1700. Centers propitious to drama were few. Cities were small. The three hundred and more nearly independent "vest-pocket" countries that comprised the Holy Roman Empire were also small. The intellectual attitudes in their courts were behind the times. Those in the Protestant north were divided from those in the Catholic south by strong antagonisms. The German language itself was spoken in multiple dialects, and progress toward a standard language was slow. It was the evolving drama that was to achieve that standard language, so that, to this day, the German equivalent of "the King's English" is *die Bühnensprache* (the stage language).

Throughout much of the century three foreign languages impeded German artistic and linguistic evolution. The aristocracy preferred to speak French, and courts imported acting troupes to provide them with the drama of Paris. Schools presented plays in Latin, chiefly imitations of Plautus and Terence, the actions of which parents and friends followed in printed German summaries. Protestant schools reluctantly began offering plays in German around 1750, but Jesuit schools stuck to Latin until 1772. The prestigious opera gave its performances in Italian. Meanwhile, rural towns and the urban poor were entertained by strolling players who doubled as jugglers, acrobats, and clowns.

Yet stage plays in German were known, most of which were prose translations of foreign works. In the 1720s professional acting companies began to take on importance. The players struggled to make a living, unaware that they were laying the foundations of the future drama of central Europe. Self-trained, recruiting members whenever and wherever, ill paid and worse treated, these men and women followed the barnstorming trail with a fierce determination. In good times they made prolonged stays at one court or in one town and ate regularly; in bad times they piled into wagons and took to the road, traveling in all weather, eating irregularly, and surviving by their wits. Arrival at a likely town meant fanfare and gaudy parade and grandiloquent proclamations. It was the opening of *I Pagliacci* in real life. And everywhere clergymen thundered against them, denouncing them as speakers of sinful lies, denying them the sacrament, refusing them Christian burial.

Audiences expected, and got, a three-act play, serious or comic, and a one-act closing skit. The play was most commonly a French classic with its verse text freely rendered in German prose and with ribald lines often gratuitously added; the skit was a ribald farce improvised as in the *commedia dell'arte*. Between the acts the clown, named Pickelhäring (Pickle Herring) or Hans Wurst (Jack Sausage), offered before-the-curtain monologues that rudely, often scatologically, parodied the adventures of the hero of the serious play.

Between 1750 and 1780 great changes came over this "German drama." Audiences gained a degree of sophistication. A play became a play and something more than an excuse for gags and buffoonery. Acting careers acquired a measure, if still short of a full mea-sure, of respectability. Theater buildings were erected, several cities engaged resident companies, and the gentry might even associate with famous performers—as Cicero of old walked in public with the tragic actor Roscius.

Within the same period, specifically from 1748 to 1781, fell the lifework of Lessing, whose splendid mind consistently strove, by precept and by example, to raise German drama into art. In 1750, when he was twenty-one, his theoretical articles restated the old claim for a moral drama in French classical forms. His articles from 1754 to 1758 were critical of the French classical forms and favored prose plays about middle-class people. In his own first full-length play, *Miss Sara Sampson* (1755), he followed the example of *The London Merchant*—but added a few touches from Congreve. This portion of his theoretical and creative work, timid and tentative as it may seem, announced the ascendancy of the bourgeois spirit over the traditional aristocratic one.

The very foundation of German drama is dated by some people from Lessing's next play, *Minna von Barnhelm* (1767), the sole German comedy of merit in its century and the oldest viable piece in the modern German repertory. This model comedy was followed in 1772 by his model tragedy, *Emilia Galotti*, which he painstakingly transposed in time from the Virginia story in Livy's *History of Rome*, each action of which he worked out in answer to his own repeated question: What would be the modern-day equivalent of this point? Immediate success attended this "Virginia in modern dress," and its influence was extensive and international. If Lessing's masterpiece, *Nathan the Wise* (1779), long remained a closet drama, its use of blank verse set the cadence for German-language dramatists, with few exceptions, until the 1860s.

Lessing's mature critical writings opened further perspectives. In No. 17 of the *Literary Letters* (1759), he proposed Shakespeare as a model for German dramatists. When, in 1767, drama enthusiasts in Hamburg built a new National Theater to replace the dilapidated opera house, Lessing began a series of reviews of selected plays, later collected in the book *The Hamburg Dramaturgy* (1767–69). In those essays, which are hardly conventional reviews, we find reasoned arguments against the three unities, against *bienséance*, against a misinterpreted Aristotle; in short, the demolition of neoclassical form and the bases for a new dramatic art.

In the 1770s German theaters were subsisting primarily on the repertory already consigned to oblivion by *The Hamburg Dramaturgy*, but novelty was introduced with a series of eccentric prose plays now collectively termed "storm-and-stress" works—from the catchy title of Maximilian Klinger's success of 1776, *Storm and Stress (Sturm und Drang)*.

The fashion was set by the young Goethe's *Götz von Berlichingen* (1774), the only artistically valid play in the lot. In the name of Shakespeare, this prose drama broke every classical rule. Instead of twenty-four hours maximum story time, it encompasses a period of years; instead of a single stage set, it has fifty-six scene changes; instead of seven to ten aristocratic roles, it uses some twenty named characters and scores of extras from all social classes. The old decorum (*bienséance*) is shattered by onstage violence, sound effects, and the broadest variety of language. For the unity of action it substitutes a Shakespearean interlocking of two plots. Its subject is a real personage from sixteenth-century German history, not a Greek or a Roman.

Most of the storm-and-stress plays are justly forgotten, but we mention two of them for their special relevance to Schiller: J. A. Leisewitz's *Julius of Taranto* (*Julius von Tarent*) and the drama plagiarized from it by Klinger, *The Twins (Die Zwillinge)*, both works of 1776. In the former, two brothers Julius and Guido, are both in love with a lady named Blanca; the jealous Guido murders Julius, their outraged father murders Guido, Blanca goes insane, and the father abdicates his princedom to become a Carthusian monk. Klinger presents twin brothers, Guelfo and Ferdinando, who quarrel over the same girl; Guelfo stabs Ferdinando, then, with his hand on the corpse, boasts of the deed to his father; the father, in horror, plunges a dagger into Guelfo.

By 1780 the youthful storm-and-stress authors had abandoned literature. The novelty of the 1780 drama season was Baron von Gemmingen's *Der deutsche Hausvater*, which closely followed Diderot's *Le Père de famille* of 1758—even to the title—and dealt with a *mésalliance* between an aristocrat and a commoner. Storm-and-stress, like a flash flood, had receded, leaving German drama about where it had been in 1770.

1. Schiller's Career as a Dramatist

Through 1781, however, Friedrich Schiller was writing *The Robbers*, with which play storm-and-stress took a new lease on life. Schiller was two months past his twenty-first birthday when he attended the premiere on January 13, 1782. An eyewitness reports:

> The theater was like a madhouse, with eyes rolling, fists clenched, and hoarse outcries through the audience. Strangers fell sobbing into each other's arms; women on the verge of fainting staggered to the door.

The universal furor was like a chaos from the mists of which a new Creation blazes forth.

Singlehanded Schiller was to prolong storm-and-stress through a second play, *Fiesco* (1784), and a third, *Intrigue and Love* (1784), and through the initial stages of a fourth, *Don Carlos*, but four distressful years of psychological and artistic change had to be lived through before that work could be completed. With the 1787 publication of *Don Carlos: A Dramatic Poem* (in blank verse), the storm-and-stress movement ends and Schiller emerges as a great dramatic poet.

Then, for ten years Schiller wrote no more plays, although plans for at least three occupied him from time to time. To that decade belong his historical writings, his professorship in history at the University of Jena, his marriage, the birth of two of his four children, the greatest number of his poems, his critical essays, one ambitious attempt at a prose narrative, his ventures into journalism, and staggering amounts of bread-and-butter editorial work.

From the composition of his *History of the Thirty Years' War* (1791—93) arose the mighty trilogy of plays collectively entitled *Wallenstein*, which occupied him from 1796 to 1799. Meanwhile, in 1794, there had begun his famous friendship with Goethe, who was manager and impresario of the Weimar Theater. In December of 1798 Schiller moved to Weimar to be closer both to Goethe and to the theater where, unofficially, he was now the poet in residence.

Exhilaration from success with his Wallenstein plays led him directly to his next drama, *Mary Stuart* (1800), and thence to *The Maid of Orleans* (1801), *The Bride of Messina* (1803), and *William Tell* (1804). Concurrently he created verse translations of

Shakespeare's *Macbeth*, Gozzi's *Turandot*, Racine's *Phèdre*, and lesser pieces. Through March and April of 1805, two acts of *Demetrius* were completed in semifinal form, but death, with brutal suddenness, overtook the poet on May 9, 1805.

2. The Man behind the Works

How Schiller, at age twenty-one, had accumulated the skills and resources to compose *The Robbers* is something of a mystery. Born in 1759, he had spent his first thirteen years in various small towns of the Duchy of Württemberg with his parents and sisters. His father, Johann Kaspar Schiller, a career officer in the army of Duke Charles Eugene, was doggedly loyal to his sovereign, stern but not cruel, and sufficiently pious to write out and preserve the family prayers he himself composed. During the last two decades of his life Captain Schiller's "military" duties consisted of managing the ducal gardens at the palace called Solitude, a short distance west of the capital city of Stuttgart. In 1795, a year before his death, he published, at his famous son's expense, a treatise on arboriculture. About Schiller's mother little is known save that she was an innkeeper's daughter. Indeed, Schiller's own childhood is singularly obscure.

At age thirteen (1773) the boy was sent, against his father's wishes but at the demand of Duke Charles Eugene, to the tuition-free ducal school at Solitude and bidden by the Duke himself to study law. At age fifteen, when the school was removed to Stuttgart, the lad chose to transfer to medical studies, apparently because he had neglected his law work and could no longer catch up. A month short of his seventeenth birthday, he had a first poem, entitled *Evening*, pub-

lished in *The Swabian Magazine*. Just past his twentieth birthday, in February, 1780, he played the title
role in Goethe's *Clavigo*, with Goethe in the audience;
a school friend reports that his acting was grotesquely
amateurish and his delivery of lines pure rant.

By the autumn of 1780 he was at work on *The
Robbers*, which was published in June, 1781. In December, 1781, upon completion of his medical course,
he was appointed regimental surgeon in a grenadier
regiment stationed in Stuttgart. A month after that, on
January 13, 1782, he witnessed the amazing premiere
of *The Robbers* at Mannheim.

To attend that premiere the young regimental surgeon absented himself without permission from his
post and traveled beyond the borders of Württemberg, for Mannheim lay in the Rhenish Palatinate. In
May, with *Fiesco* already in composition, he made the
journey to Mannheim again, in the mistaken belief
that *The Robbers* was being given a second performance, but this time his absence without leave was
brought to the attention of the duke, who imposed
two weeks' detention upon the offender, probably
June 28 to July 12, 1782. The exasperating inaction of
that confinement gave rise to the idea for a third play,
"Luise Miller," ultimately to be called *Intrigue and
Love*, which would portray Duke Charles Eugene for
all posterity as a knave and a fool. In August the duke
was irritated afresh when the Swiss canton of Grisons
protested a phrase in *The Robbers* (II, 3) that named
their region "the Athens of modern scoundrels." On
threat of imprisonment in Hohenasperg Fortress, the
duke forbade his regimental surgeon to write any
more plays. The threat was very real. The writer
Schubart had offended the duke in 1776 and had been
in Hohenasperg ever since—without trial. Schiller interrupted work on *Fiesco* to compose a letter of self-

defense, dated September 1, but the letter was not accepted and the duke instructed that no more letters should be written. Schiller made up his mind to flee Württemberg at the earliest opportunity.

Three weeks later the duke was much occupied with entertaining Grand Duke Paul of Russia (later Tsar Paul I, 1796–1801), and there was Schiller's opportunity. On the evening of September 22, 1782, Schiller, under the name of "Dr. Ritter," and his musician friend Andreas Streicher, under the name of "Dr. Wolf," passed through the city gate of Stuttgart in a carriage that brought them safely to Mannheim the following day. There, theater manager Meyer was so scandalized at the defection that he obliged Schiller to write an immediate apology to the duke. A reply came a few days later from Schiller's regimental commander saying that the duke was "very favorably disposed," but the fugitive had no intention of going back.

On September 26, before Meyer and a large group of actors, including the famous Iffland, Schiller gave a reading of *Fiesco*, but so badly did he read and so thick was his Swabian dialect that a halt was called after Act II. Meyer even took Streicher aside and inquired whether this young man had actually written *The Robbers*, but he did retain the manuscript and read it privately overnight. In the morning he declared that *Fiesco* was a masterpiece and better composed than *The Robbers*. Production decisions, however, would have to await the return of the impresario, Baron Dalberg, who was attending the festivities in Stuttgart.

Even under false names the two fugitives dreaded that any moment might bring extradition agents from Württemberg, so that, with *Fiesco*'s fate undecided, they set out on foot to find safer quarters. For a couple of weeks they managed to subsist in the hamlet of Sachsenhausen, a suburb of Frankfurt, until Schiller's funds gave out, then for about six weeks in the hamlet of Oggersheim, near Mannheim, until Streicher's funds gave out. Through both periods Schiller worked eagerly away at *Intrigue and Love*, interrupting himself repeatedly to make more and ever more revisions in *Fiesco*, as demanded by Baron Dalberg's letters. Finally, at the end of his financial tether, he decided to avail himself of a refuge offered him some months previously by Henriette von Wolzogen, the mother of two school friends, at her rural estate of Bauerbach, near Meiningen in central Germany.

The stagecoach journey lasted from November 30 to December 7. The three miles or more from Meiningen to Bauerbach were covered on foot. Once at his destination, however, Schiller settled in with tolerable comfort for the rural winter and spring. There *Fiesco* and *Intrigue and Love* were both finished and *Don Carlos* begun. To Streicher and to his benefactress letters were sent, giving elaborately false information, lest the duke's spies should be watching the mails. As far as is known, the duke sent no spies. To him, apparently, one regimental surgeon less was a small loss and one writer less was no loss at all.

From Mannheim came letter after letter from Baron Dalberg, always insisting on still further revisions in *Fiesco* and in *Intrigue and Love*. At last, on July 24, 1783, impatience drove Schiller to travel to Mannheim, come what may, and confer with Dalberg in person.

The Mannheim stay, August, 1783, to April, 1785, began well and had its gratifying moments, but it ended in dissatisfaction. On January 11, 1784, *Fiesco* had a moderate success—with a conciliatory ending contrary to the dramatist's intention. In April of the same year *Intrigue and Love* had great success. In December, Act I of *Don Carlos*, in prose, was given a reading in Darmstadt in the presence of Duke Charles Augustus of Weimar, who granted Schiller the title of Weimar councillor and a small pension. These triumphs were gratifying, and they paid some, but not all, of the bills. Moreover, relations with Baron Dalberg were becoming gradually uncomfortable. There were differences with some of the Mannheim actors, particularly Iffland. In private life there were unsuccessful little forays into the domain of the heart's affections. What Schiller had hoped for was a regularized position that would permit him to write plays for a congenial impresario and a troupe of congenial players, but the longer he stayed in Mannheim, the further that hope receded from him.

In June, 1784, Schiller had received an extraordinary gift from four unknown persons in eastern Germany: Christian Gottfried Körner and Ludwig Ferdinand Huber and their fiancées, the Stock sisters. The gift consisted of four letters full of praise for his published plays, an embroidered letter case, a poem, and signed portraits of the four well-wishers. Deeply touched as he was, Schiller allowed six distracted months to pass before writing a reply, but soon after his letter, there came Körner's invitation to come to Leipzig. In April, 1785, Körner's generosity made it possible to accept that invitation, and Schiller left Mannheim with no regrets.

The two-year period in eastern Germany, first in Leipzig and then in Dresden, began auspiciously and ended in frustration, repeating the pattern of the Mannheim years. *Don Carlos*, already under composition for two years, was proving extraordinarily difficult to compose, and two more years would be spent at it before its completion in blank-verse form in 1787. A distressful psychological maturation was in progress. There were private frustrations. Above all, neither Leipzig nor Dresden offered the chance to work with a congenial impresario and a troupe of congenial players. Had it not been for Körner's steadfast friendship, Schiller might have despaired.

In the summer of 1787 he set off on what he intended to be an extensive tour around Germany, his manuscripts and writing materials so packed as to be available for daily use. Actually, the itinerary did not take him further than various towns in the province of Thuringia, but it resulted in acquaintance with the two sisters von Lengefeld, both of whom held attractions for him. For some time he kept up correspondence with both of them, but gradually he came to reject the intellectual, novel-writing, older Karoline in favor of the less pretentious, younger Charlotte. In a letter of January 7, 1788, he told Körner: "All creatures to whom I have attached myself have had something dearer to them than I. . . . Only marriage is left as a way out." And so it proved. The epistolary wooing of Charlotte von Lengefeld came to a betrothal in August, 1789, and to marriage on February 22, 1790. At age thirty he had found himself a faithful, if dull, wife, to whom he in turn was faithful.

Finances had meanwhile improved. In addition to his daily stint of bread-and-butter writing and editing, Schiller had been nominated by Goethe in December, 1788, for a professorship in history at the University of Jena, and on May 26, 1789, he had given his maiden lecture there. Just prior to his marriage, the Duke of Weimar had increased his pension. In December, 1791, certain Danish admirers obtained for him a small annual stipend from the king of Denmark.

Even as he was becoming economically secure, however, his health showed signs of giving way. January, 1791, brought a serious lung infection, the first declaration of the malady that would eventually cause his death in the middle of his forty-sixth year. A second attack in May, 1791, brought him close to death. A third attack in January, 1792, kept him for weeks in bed. Ultimately, he had to give up his professorship on account of the bad health.

There were compensatory gratifications. In 1793, Schiller was able to go, with his wife, on an extended journey back to the scenes of his childhood. A son was born to them during their stay in Stuttgart. At roughly the same time, his old enemy, Duke Charles Eugene of Württemberg, happened to die (October 24, 1793) at the end of a long reign. At his old school, Schiller was accorded an enthusiastic reception. He was, in short, a well-known author and a famous man.

Yet all through those years from 1789 to 1794 Schiller was not in his proper element. The dreamed-of theater position did not materialize and a great dramatic poet was lying fallow. By the most regrettable of ironies, both for Schiller and for posterity, the ideal impresario in the person of Goethe and the ideal theater existed, existed only a few miles from Jena, where Schiller now lived, and yet an invisible barrier kept him away until July, 1794. From that point until his death in 1805, his life—his essential life—was to be his association with Goethe and the Weimar Theater.

3. Goethe

Back in February, 1780, the thirty-one-year-old Goethe had watched that school performance of his play *Clavigo* in which Schiller, three months past age twenty, passionately tore the title role to tatters, making himself and the hero ridiculous. The impression was unfortunate and long-lasting. What is more, Schiller's meteoric rise as a dramatist from 1782 to 1784 disheartened Goethe. He himself had abjured storm-and-stress literature and storm-and-stress life style in 1775. Those works he believed to be bad for the writers and bad for the public. He had observed with relief how the flash flood of storm-and-stress had abated by 1780. And then, in the early 1780s, along had come Schiller and wrongheadedly started the whole process anew.

As adults, the two authors first met on September 7, 1788, at the home of Schiller's future wife in Rudolstadt, and on that occasion Schiller was on his guard and Goethe displayed all the warmth of an iceberg. Two weeks later, Schiller published his hostile review of Goethe's *Egmont*. Yet in December, Goethe, as rector of the University of Jena, proposed Schiller for a professorship there. One suspects he was bending over backward to be fair. Upon receiving the news, Schiller traveled to Weimar to pay Goethe a formal thank-you call; the interview was correct and cold. A month later, January, 1789, Schiller published his review of Goethe's *Iphigenia in Tauris*, a kinder article than the *Egmont* review but still reserved. Not until October, 1790, did Goethe return Schiller's call by traveling to Jena to visit him; they discussed Kant and parted on much the same terms as before. For the next three and a half years Schiller kept steadily to his own work, determined not to press an unwanted friendship.

As honorary members of the Jena Scientific Society both of them attended meetings of that organization from July 20 to July 23, 1794, and following one of the sessions they got into a conversation about certain concepts of botanical evolution. At some point in the conversation their mutual and undeclared antagonism began to thaw in the warmth of common interests.

Exchange of letters began on July 25 and rapidly became a running stream of discussion of each other's works and plans and ideas. Schiller was for the last two weeks of September Goethe's invited guest in Weimar.

Schiller, on his part, disclosed that he had plans for both a Wallenstein drama and a Knights of Malta drama. Goethe encouraged the former, with the result that Schiller began work on his Wallenstein trilogy, the first installment of which served for the gala opening of the new theater in Weimar on October 12, 1798. The following year Schiller moved to Weimar: he had found both his impresario and his acting troupe, and therewith he had found his rightful place. He was now thirty-five.

4. The Weimar Theater

The theater for which Schiller's major plays were composed was the public theater managed by Goethe for Duke Charles Augustus, partially subsidized by the duke for the entertainment of himself and his court but at the same time operated with an eye to box-office success and open to all the duke's subjects insofar as they were able to afford a ticket. Thus, it conjoined two dramatic worlds: the old one, in which a prince specified and paid for his court's entertainment by "comedians," and the new one, in which a mixed public paid its own way and in the long run determined the dramatic fare. Goethe's managerial position had resulted from evolving circumstances.

The craze for amateur theatricals among the French nobility of the 1760s had caught on with the German nobility of the 1770s, so that Goethe, upon arrival in Weimar in 1775, soon became the unofficial master of the revels in charge of various kinds of court entertainments. Masquerade balls were at first his specialty, but he went on to compose plays and playlets and operetta libretti, to supervise their production, and not infrequently to function as an actor in them. A single cast might bring together professional actors and singers, courtiers and government functionaries participating as amateurs, and even the duke himself—all gladly collaborating with their poet-director and fellow performer. Meanwhile, a local commercial theater offered standard repertory pieces to courtiers and general public alike.

When, in 1791, the duke created his own theater and made it open to the public, Goethe accepted the post of manager with misgivings. The conventional repertory offered little challenge, but, as was his nature, he tended seriously to business. He was to continue at that job for twenty-six years, until 1817. Once the friendship with Schiller was established after 1794, Goethe soon saw that he might realize his own long-cherished ambition of operating a theater where great drama could be created. No longer need he be restricted to second-rate repertory works; now he could collaborate with a theater-poet with ideals as high as his own, and yet a practical poet, for all of that. Before Schiller's dramatic genius he bowed, himself contributing only one new play—the coldly received *Natural Daughter* (1803)—but bending all efforts to see that his friend's works received optimum performances.

By a happy chance, Schiller's first new offering coincided with the opening of a brand-new theater—hence the 138-line prologue that heads the *Wallenstein* text. The new structure seated five hundred persons comfortably, although as many as eight hundred might squeeze in for that favorite of favorites, Mozart's *Magic Flute*. In the middle of the first balcony was the ducal loge; to its right sat the nobles, and to its left sat the court functionaries. Better-class commoners occupied the ground floor, at the rear of which Goethe had his box, directly below the ducal loge. There he sometimes offered cream tarts to small children during intermission. Working-class persons were accommodated in the second balcony.

The inclined plane of the stage was forty feet square, with a thirty-six-foot-wide proscenium arch and with five wings of scenery at either side; the backdrop had to be rolled up by hand. For the first time oil lamps served as footlights, so that Goethe no longer needed to snuff the footlight candles, as a poem of his complains of having occasionally had to do. A cluster of oil lamps above the audience could be hoisted into a ceiling recess to produce semidarkness in the hall. Sergeants-at-arms maintained order, and improper behavior, such as hissing, resulted in immediate arrest. The audience was, after all, in the presence of its absolute sovereign and, in a sense, they were guests in his house. Applause was normally withheld until the duke applauded.

Of this theater Goethe was both manager and impresario, receiving upward of one-third of costs in subsidy from the duke but otherwise insisting on budgetary economies and on plays that would pay their own way. Upon the players he imposed professional and personal discipline. He could be kindly and tactful, especially with older performers, but when an eighteen-year-old actress undertook an engagement in Berlin without permission, he ordered a week's house arrest and obliged her to pay out of her own pocket for the sentry posted at her door. His ideal was a troupe working as a team, without stars, all using a standard pronunciation and trained in the statuesque

Dignity (*Über Anmut und Würde*; 1793) and *On Naive and Sentimental Poetry* (*Über naive und sentimentalische Dichtung*; 1795), the latter dealing with the vexed question of classical and romantic ideals in art. Many people find these essays to be Schiller's most important contributions to the history of ideas.

6. Schiller's Personality

If Schiller himself could not act, he could show others how. By his warmth and charm he could also coax sullen players to better efforts when Goethe could do nothing with them. When Goethe almost canceled the *Macbeth* premiere because the leading man, Vohs, had not learned his lines, Schiller insisted the show go on, and Vohs acquitted himself quite well. Backstage, Schiller embraced him, exclaiming in his usual Swabian accent: "*Meischterhaft! Meischterhaft!*" ("masterful"), and to his friend Genast, he added: "*Sehe Sie, Genascht, wir habe recht gehabt! Er hat zwar andere Vers gesproche, als ich geschriebe habe, aber er ischt trefflich!*" ("You see, Genast, we were right! It's true he spoke different lines from what I wrote, but he's fine!")

Once Goethe accepted Schiller as a friend and collaborator, their relationship remained cordial and immensely productive artistically. After Schiller's death Goethe found himself looking back upon his friend with ever deepening awe. Twenty-five years later, in 1830, in a private letter, he compared Schiller to Christ.

Reminiscences *de mortuis* are not always informative. That Dr. Riemer, Goethe's one-time secretary, recalled Schiller's proud stance and gait and his gentle eyes, tells us little. That Dr. Riemer also found him

techniques of the French classical drama. He marked off the stage with chalk and rehearsed his players in every move and stance. With a company that doubled as actors and singers, he put on operas and operettas on Tuesdays, classics and experimental works on Thursdays, and light comedies on Saturdays—when the best people were away for the weekend and when the lads from the University of Jena might be a trifle freer.

The opening night at this new building saw *Wallenstein's Camp*. Here on January 30, 1799, *The Piccolomini* was first given for the duchess's birthday, an anniversary usually marked by some special performance. Here *The Bride of Messina*, on March 19, 1803, elicited cheers from the Jena students, who next day were reprimanded by school authorities for their disrespect toward their sovereign. And here, a month later, on April 23, the players took double and triple roles to account for the large cast of *The Maid of Orleans*. For that production there was purchased, after insistence by both Goethe and Schiller, an imitation-velvet coronation robe, which then did duty for a series of other stage monarchs. Here were performed Schiller's translations of *Macbeth*, *Turandot*, and *Phèdre*, as well as of two French comedies by Louis Benoît Picard (1769–1825), for the duke had requested them, not wishing to have his theater always serious. Here *William Tell* was launched on its spectacular career on March 17, 1804. Here Shakespeare's *Julius Caesar*, in the splendid new translation by August Wilhelm Schlegel, was coolly received in 1803 by an audience that found it disturbingly remote from neoclassical principles. Here two plays of Terence were presented in experimental performances using masks. Here Friedrich Schlegel's *Ion* caused titters, which Goethe, rising from his box, shushed. And here, again and again, *The Magic Flute* packed the house, despite the small orchestra and the players, who were only tolerable singers.

The Weimar Theater was not the Globe or Versailles or the Athenian Theater of Dionysus, but in those seven years from 1798 to 1805 it was listed among the immortal stages of the world. The patron duke approved the work of his two collaborating geniuses, commoners kept the box office solvent, and illiterates are reported to have memorized whole speeches from Schiller's plays. The town of Weimar then had a population of around five thousand, but it supported an artistic enterprise of worldwide significance.

5. Schiller's Nondramatic Works

Nine dramas—eleven, if the three parts of *Wallenstein* are counted separately—constitute the crown of Schiller's career; ideas for as many more remain as fascinating sketches attesting a unique imagination at work. Long cherished in equal esteem, and still cherished by many, are the poems, which easily fill a volume. To music lovers the *Ode to Joy* (*An die Freude*) is familiar from the finale of Beethoven's *Ninth Symphony*, as the later elegy *Nänie* is familiar from a fine setting by Brahms. "Idea poems," such as *The Gods of Greece* (*Die Götter Griechenlands*) and *The Dignity of Women* (*Würde der Frauen*), are conspicuous among Schiller's verse, while ideas on a wide range of topics form the subjects of about a hundred pithy epigrams, most often cast in the two-line mold of the Latin heroic couplet. Most famous of all the poems are the fifteen or so ballads, story-poems such as *The Glove* (*Der Handschuh*), *The Cranes of*

Ibykus (*Die Kraniche des Ibykus*), and *The* (*Der Taucher*), which are miniature *Novelle* often illustrative of a moral precept.

The prose works are voluminous. A handful of from the 1780s, strike a certain journalistic ton betoken Schiller's concern with psychological ana *The Game of Fate* (*Das Spiel des Schicksals*) de from life, a cruel commander of a prison; *A Remark Case of a Woman's Revenge* retells, from Diderot with a shift of emphasis, the story of a lady who p ished an unfaithful lover by contriving his marri with a "reformed" prostitute; *Criminal from Loss Honor* (*Der Verbrecher aus verlorener Ehre*) plores the life of a man who turns to crime only af society has destroyed his self-respect. On a larg scale, *The Ghost-seer* (*Der Geisterseher*; 1789 which was planned for novel length but left unfi ished, deals with intrigue and secret societies in colorfully mysterious Venice.

The extensive historical writings of the year 1787–93 include articles on various topics, such as the account of Count Egmont's trial and the Jesuit regime in Paraguay, but they culminate in the full-length studies, *The Revolt of the Netherlands* (*Geschichte des Abfalls der vereinigten Niederlande von der spanischen Regierung*; 1788) and *History of the Thirty Years' War* (*Geschichte des dreyßigjährigen Kriegs*; 1791–93). Investigations have revealed that these works were elaborately researched, and if some critics have found them too poetical for sober history or others have deemed them prejudiced by philosophical theory, they remain eminently readable as well as important for more than the background of *Don Carlos* and *Wallenstein*. Most significant of the prose writings are the essays devoted, in the 1790s, to the philosophy of esthetics, particularly *On Grace and*

desultory, may perhaps relate to Schiller's repeated taking up and repeated putting aside of dramatic projects. Appointments fretted Schiller, Goethe recalled, and unexpected visits unnerved him. In November, 1802, Duke Charles Augustus elevated him to aristocratic rank, with the name of Friedrich von Schiller. Doubtless Schiller was gratified, but his reference to the matter in a letter of 1803 speaks only of his wife's delight in flouncing about the court with a train to her dress. When the king of Sweden sent him a diamond ring, he remarked that these gentlemen of state set great store by such items, "but our kingdom is not of this world." A second diamond sent him by the tsaritsa of Russia he sold to pay off a mortgage. More startling is that story Goethe recounted to Eckermann on October 7, 1827, about how he once waited in Schiller's study. The air was foul and Goethe began to be nauseated. Searching about, he opened a desk drawer and found it full of rotten apples. Mrs. Schiller explained that her husband could not live or write unless he had that odor around him.

These random traits suggest more than the bland image conveyed by the biographical tradition of Schiller. One glimpses a rare but troubled spirit. His life, apart from touches of melodrama in 1782, was unspectacular. It was a life earth-bound, with unremitting work and petty frustrations, but in his dramas there is always a soaring exaltation.

THE PLAYS

The Robbers

As the work of a dramatist in his twentieth and twenty-first years, *The Robbers* (*Die Räuber*) is amazing, not only for being eminently stageworthy but for its anticipation of surrealist techniques still far in the future. It presents only emotionally intense scenes, leaving antecedent action and many transitions to be inferred. Of two overlapping strata of story, one is a family drama set in Franconia, in western Germany, the other, a drama of young desperadoes who operate as a band of highwaymen in various vaguely defined regions of eastern Germany. The bandit leader is Karl von Moor, who, in Acts IV and V, returns with his bandits to the native regions whence he was wrongfully exiled.

In the family story, the reigning Count von Moor is elderly, infirm, well-intentioned, and weak-willed. In the absence of his older son Karl, he lives domineered by his younger son, Franz, who covets both his brother's inheritance and his brother's beloved Amalia, a young woman who lives at the castle as a member of the family. Franz's accomplice in evil is another member of the household, one Hermann, whose identity is never declared but whom we infer to be the count's

natural son. (These relationships bring to mind Dostoevsky's Karamazov father, the Karamazov sons Dmitri
and Ivan, and the illegitimate half-brother Smerdya-
kov.)

As the play begins, Franz is tormenting his father
with a forged letter from Karl describing the latter's
debauched and lawless existence in eastern Germany.
It is Franz's reply, made in his father's name, which, in
Act I, Scene 2, makes Karl resolve to lead a highwayman's life. In I, 3 Franz presses his unwelcome suit
upon Amalia and is rebuffed. Working then on some
unexplained grievance of Hermann's, Franz persuades
Hermann to impersonate a messenger bringing the report of Karl's death in battle in the Seven Years' War
(1756–63), at which news the count apparently dies
of shock.

In III, 1, a garden scene, Franz presses his attentions
anew upon Amalia, but the mettlesome girl slaps him,
and when he attempts to seize her by force, she ac-
cedes just long enough to get possession of his sword,
with which she holds him at bay. When he has retired,
Hermann, stricken with remorse, comes to Amalia and
declares that neither Karl nor her uncle, the count, is
really dead.

Act IV opens with Karl's return home in disguise.
Belatedly, Franz identifies him and bullies the old servant Daniel into a promise to murder the visitor (IV,
2), but the faithful old retainer has also penetrated the
stranger's disguise and warns Karl in good time
(IV, 3).

In IV, 5 Karl and his robbers are encamped in a
forest near an old castle tower—how they made their
way across Germany is not clear—and there the
awakening Karl discovers Hermann in the act of
bringing food secretly to a prisoner in the old ruin.
The prisoner is Count von Moor. At his apparent

death from shock the count's body had been placed in a coffin, but on the way to burial he had revived and scratched on the coffin lid. Franz opened the coffin, cried out, "Do you mean to live forever?" and slammed the lid shut again. To avoid outright murder, Franz had then conveyed him to this tower, intending to let him die of starvation. Karl now sets the prisoner free, but, though he recognizes him as his father, maintains his own incognito. He fires a shot to rouse his men and sends them to seize Franz and bring him to the camp alive.

In V, 1, however, Franz wakes in terror from a premonitory dream of his own judgment after death. He sends the astonished old retainer Daniel to fetch Pastor Moser—based on the Pastor Philipp Ulrich Moser, whom the boy Schiller had admired in the town of Lorch—but Moser's solemn words only increase Franz's terror. When Karl's robbers are heard approaching, Franz hangs himself.

Although the robbers failed to capture Franz alive, they capture Amalia as she seeks to flee the castle. Karl greets her with joy but still does not betray his incognito. When his companions reproach him for the intention of abandoning them for this woman and thereby breaking his sworn oath of loyalty to them, Karl slays Amalia with his own hand. In the midst of this turmoil, the old count has quietly expired. The play will presently end with Karl's surrender to the civil law and to execution, and therewith the family will be annihilated.

The robbers plot begins with Act I, Scene 2, in a tavern on the borders of Saxony. How Karl chances to be there we are not told, and we are left to infer that his companions are restless and impoverished youths, with some degree of learning and with much devotion to him. When Franz's impudent letter is delivered, announcing that Count von Moor will never forgive his older son, the companions propose to organize themselves into a robber band with Karl as leader.

The long Scene 3 of Act II finds the band deep in the Bohemian Forest and encircled by vastly superior forces of militia. When a haughty pater (Catholic priest) is sent in to them to dictate surrender terms, Karl delivers a memorable tirade about the corruption among civil and religious authorities. The outraged pater offers a general amnesty if the men will deliver Karl to him as prisoner, but the men defy him and the battle begins—just as the curtain falls. In III, 2, "near the Danube," we learn that the robbers won the battle but with the loss of Roller, one of their most-valued men. Through the forest now comes a volunteer named Kosinsky, a dispossessed Bohemian nobleman whose life story parallels Karl's, even to a lost bride named Amalia.

It is with Kosinsky that Karl comes in disguise to his native castle (IV, 1) and holds a conversation with Amalia in the family portrait gallery (IV, 2). Both Karl and Kosinsky escape (IV, 3) after the old servant Daniel's timely warning, yet even after that Karl returns, still in disguise, for a tryst with Amalia in the garden (IV, 4).

The fourth act ends with the nocturnal scene (5) in which Karl delivers his father from the starvation tower, while V, 1 presents Franz's terror and suicide. The final scene (V, 2) portrays Karl's sacrificial murder of Amalia, the old count's death, and Karl's offer to surrender himself to the civil authorities in order to win amnesty for his followers. The men will not hear of it, and they also deride the notion of his suicide as an act of egotistical bravura. In his final speech Karl scorns any death that will result in admiration for himself.

> "I remember [he says] talking on my way over here
> with a poor devil of a day-laborer with eleven chil-
> dren. A thousand louis d'or have been offered to who-
> ever brings in the great robber alive.—That man can
> be helped."

Sources

A benign father who beholds with horror the fratri-
cidal hatred of his two sons, rivalry of two brothers
for the love of the same girl, extinction of a family
(and of a dynasty): these elements are common to
The Robbers and to that pair of storm-and-stress plays
of 1776, Leisewitz's *Julius of Taranto* and Klinger's
The Twins. Aspects of what we term the family story
have been traced to a prose narrative by C. F. D.
Schubart, *In the History of the Human Heart,* which
appeared in the January, 1775, issue of *The Swabian
Magazine.* Ultimately, the basic situation of a good
father with a trusted bad son and a mistrusted good
son betokens an influence from the Gloucester subplot
of *King Lear,* while echoes of Richard III's opening
monologue are heard in Franz's monologue in Act I:

> ". . . I have good reasons to be angry with Nature . . .
> Why did she have to load me with this burden of
> ugliness? Me! As if at my birth she spawned a rem-
> nant. Why a Lapplander's nose on *me*? And this black-
> amoor's fuzz? These Hottentot eyes? Honestly, I think
> she tossed the hideous features from all human species
> in a pile and baked me from them . . ."

Characters

Indeed, Franz has been diagnosed as a Richard III with a conscience. Unloved, ugly, and alone, he is a luckless villain, frustrated in his greed for the inheritance as in his love suit. After debating (II, 1) methods of shortening his father's life without resort to outright murder, and after deciding for terror-shock, he invents nothing more shocking than the false report of Karl's death. For the moment the device seems adequate, but then comes the adventure with the coffin. One half-measure failing, he resorts to the second half-measure of the starvation tower—shades of Ugolino!—only to yield up his entire enterprise when he has a horrid dream of after-death judgment. Franz is unpleasant but not mean enough by half.

Of Karl, Schiller said that he was "not a scoundrel, not a monster," but we never suspected he was. He is handsome, in contrast to his ugly brother. He is ever surrounded by friends, just as Franz is ever alone. He is loyal to the core, as any hero of Schiller's must be. Significantly he feels immediate sympathy for a fellow nobleman, Kosinsky. He is capable of action but is not primarily a man of action. Rather, he is a meditative idealist who is driven to desperate action by the injustice and corruption of society. Still, he is a somber master who works his will with people, even to the slaying of his betrothed Amalia when he sees she may never be his. His self-disgust is a crucial point in a hero who otherwise anticipates the world-weary Byronic hero.

Amalia is a paragon of maidenly virtues, unexpectedly endowed with the spunk to offer physical counteroffense to the offensive Franz. It is odd that her feminine intuition should not divine Karl's identity as the two of them stand together in the family portrait gallery, but recognition would not serve the dramatist's intentions. Baron Dalberg of the Mannheim Theater urged Schiller to allow her to survive, but Schiller was adamant: Karl must himself destroy his last temptation to live.

The old count and the servant Daniel are stock characters. Hermann, potentially so interesting, is forced into a role of contradictions and ineffectuality. The seven robber companions, plus Kosinsky, are quickly but effectively distinguished from one another in the very brief space possible, the sardonic nihilist Spiegelberg being the most memorable of them.

The Play as a Whole

Through the first three acts the individual scenes readily play, while the two plots alternate in contrasting settings. In Act IV the separate plots merge but the settings continue to contrast in indoor and outdoor scenes. Only in the portrait gallery do we see Karl within his home walls, where, significantly, he comes disguised as a stranger. It is striking that the two brothers never meet on stage. In fact, an ambitious actor could play both roles if his voice could stand the strain. Such deliberate avoidance of confrontation suggests a parallel portrayal of two worlds, the private one and the public one, with the hero essaying to cope with the corruption in each. In any case, Schiller's concern was not with a vendetta between two brothers as private individuals.

The language of The Robbers is both villain and hero. By modern standards the characters rant. The poetic component is slight. This youthful dramatist was in love with words and he set his characters talking with the greatest enthusiasm. The monologues of Franz are verbal *tours de force*, triumphantly stage-worthy—if overlong. But in them there is more fire-works than humanity. They are not nearly so devilish as he and the dramatist intend them to be. Spiegel-berg's long tirade in II, 3, about how he and his cronies plundered a convent and raped all the nuns for the sheer sport of it, is a unique case of off-color humor on Schiller's part, but it also vividly establishes a char-acter. The humor, we add, was facile in arch-Protes-tant circles.

Religiosity pervades this text, a religiosity that may be fairly described as partisan and naïve, even to the dead-earnest solemnity of Pastor Moser as opposed to the infuriating arrogance of the pater. This is Protes-tant spite at its meanest, and the author is—regrettably —sincere about it, just as he is sincere in "thinking" his text in terms of evangelical exhortation. Schiller was not the first youthful poet to "howl," nor the last, but when he sets Karl to castigating the ills of society, he makes him answer the pater with the fervent over-simplifications of a parish preacher. The confrontation is no less effective for all that because it opposes, with flamboyant rhetoric, everlasting Hypocrisy and ever-lasting Honesty; for a few minutes the pater and Karl take on mythic proportions.

It is altogether a remarkable scene, that II, 3. It is built up with dramatic sureness, from Spiegelberg's tirades, to the story of Roller's capture and deliver-ance, which rings in the never-failing motif of loyal comrades pitching in to rescue one lost man, and on the confrontation with the pater, the whole long scene ending just as decisive battle against heavy odds is about to begin. Thomas Mann was right in terming this "glorified cowboys and Indians" (*das höhere In-dianerspiel*), but it gives more dramatic pleasure than the story of meanness in castle halls. The emphasis, however, is not on swashbuckling adventure, although that is present, too, but on the moral oratory from the woodland pulpit.

Stage History

In that psychologically shattering premiere of 1782 the famous actor Iffland played the role of Franz as the leading role in a grandiose moral melodrama, and for the rest of the century star actors followed his example. In the early nineteenth century, the great romantic actor Ludwig Devrient also played Franz, interpreting him as an aristocratic satan of a man. In terms of English stage history, the role passed, as it were, from David Garrick to Edmund Kean. By 1836 leading actors had come to see Karl as the primary role, and directors stressed the wildwood lair of romantic outlaws. Large numbers of soldier extras were introduced and real gunpowder was used to produce the sound of cannonfire. In the realistic era of the 1870s and 1880s, intellectuals were generally cool to the work, but in 1889 Theodor Fontane, the novelist, who had written off the role of Karl as unplayable, was astonished at Adalbert Matkowsky's interpretation, which alternated styles "from thunderstorm to nightingale-song, from Icelandic berserker-stuff to jasmine-arbor sentimentality." Particularly startling was Karl's ghastly and prolonged scream as his father emerged from the starvation tower.

Twentieth-century productions have tended to concentrate on the play as a whole. Max Reinhardt's version of 1908 moved the robbers as a chorus group in a spectacularly vast forest, but it also made more of the role of Amalia. Erwin Piscator's 1926 version radically cut the family story to expand the robbers story into a contemporary play about political revolutionaries, even to the making of the "genuine" revolutionary Spiegelberg more important than Karl von Moor. Since 1959 productions have often used aggressively stylized sets and indulged specialized notions of directors.

Modern readers and audiences are likely to see *The Robbers* either as a parable of revolution or as a flight from urban misery to the pleasant anarchy of forest brigandage. The latter may distantly resemble the life in Nottingham Forest, but it is wholly alien to life in the Forest of Arden. Schiller himself is likely to have preferred Iffland's moral castigation of life in castles.

In French translation *The Robbers* had a separate career of its own. As presented on March 10, 1792, at the Théâtre du Marais in Paris it had tremendous success even in a radically cut and altered form. There Karl, contrary to Schiller's particular wish, committed suicide out of remorse. The audience was impatient with a revolutionary who was thus remorseful over revolutionary actions in the far-off Bohemian Forest. In their city it was the paters who were being sent to the guillotine, not the sympathetic heroes. Hence, a new ending was supplied by Beaumarchais: Karl writes an explanatory letter to the emperor imploring general pardon, and just before the final curtain the emperor's messenger arrives with the pardon and transforms the robbers into legitimte protectors of authority. Robespierre, however, saw the play as a two-edged sword and forbade it. By 1799 it was again playing in Paris, in six theaters simultaneously, because Napoleon deemed it useful propaganda for his new regime.

Meanwhile, in the summer of 1792, the legislature of the French First Republic had granted the author of

The Robbers honorary citizenship in the homeland of the revolution, extending the same privilege to other foreigners: the Swiss educational reformer Pestalozzi, the Polish patriot Kosziusko, and the American president, George Washington. In 1792 this election came to a Schiller much changed from his impetuous youth, aghast at the Parisian *terreur*, and repentant for ever having composed *The Robbers* at all.

Fiesco

Schiller's second play is the "orphan" among his works for the stage. Nominally, it is a historical drama, with the full title *The Conspiracy of Fiesco in Genoa: A Republican Tragedy (Die Verschwörung des Fiesco zu Genua*), with action dated to 1547, and with personages drawn from real-life Italian history, yet the text freely alludes to manners and ideas of Schiller's own era. Characters may, for instance, anachronistically visit coffeehouses or serve hot chocolate; the Jesuits (founded in 1534) are mentioned with an Age-of-Enlightenment and Protestant antipathy; in Act III Countess Julia Doria vents her pique by stepping over to a piano and dashing off "an Allegro." Not only does the play open with a masquerade ball, but through the entire work eighteenth-century Germans masquerade as sixteenth-century Italians.

The sources, as Schiller named them in his preface, were Part III of Robertson's *History of Charles V* and certain French books, including *La Conjuration du Comte Jean-Louis de Fiesque* by the Cardinal de Retz (who was himself a dabbler in conspiracy). The historical Giovanni Luigi de' Fieschi (ca. 1523–47) was a brilliant young nobleman who, in the complex politics of Genoa, enlisted the help of Francis I of France and of the Duke of Parma to overthrow the reigning family of the Dorias, these latter being supported by Holy Roman Emperor Charles V. In so doing, Count Fiesco was only recapitulating political intrigues by which Andrea Doria had himself sought power twenty-five years earlier, in 1522, before the latter had switched sides. The uprising of January 2, 1547, went off according to plan. The city gates were seized, as were the galleys in port, and Gianettino Doria, the doge's nephew, was killed in attempting to prevent the takeover of the galleys. But the eighty-one-year-old Andrea Doria escaped. At the very moment of success, however, Fiesco fell from a boarding plank of one of the galleys and was drowned. Despite a quickly patched-up truce and amnesty, Andrea returned to arrest, put to torture, and execute the surviving conspirators. At age eighty-four he was personally commanding an expedition against Barbary pirates, and he remained a formidable warrior and statesman until his death in 1560, at age ninety-four.

The central action, as we expect, is Fiesco's conspiracy to overthrow the tyrant Andrea Doria, but to this main theme are appended three subplots, so that the overall design is intricate.

In the main plot Fiesco has slyly prepared his conspiracy by living, in the eyes of all, as a recklessly irresponsible dissolute who is incapable of any action so serious-minded as revolution making. Other Genoese citizens have their own conspiratorial plans, which are brought to a head when the doge's nephew, Gianettino Doria, violates Bertha, the daughter of stern old Verrina. Late in Act II the two conspiracies are merged into one. In the monologue that concludes that act, Fiesco debates with himself whether he will be the savior of a republican Genoa or the new tyrant duke. He decides to be the republican savior. In III, 2 he debates the issue anew—and decides to make himself the next tyrant duke.

In the thick of the fray in Act V he does proclaim himself duke publicly and in the final scene appears before Verrina in ducal regalia. To the true republican Verrina this is monstrous. He refuses even private friendship with the usurper, saying, "The first Prince was a murderer and introduced the purple to hide the stains of his deed in the color of blood." With profound irony he steps back in deference to the "superior" Fiesco and allows him to pass first across the gangplank to the galley they are boarding. Midway across he wrenches the ducal cloak from Fiesco's shoulders and in the ensuing scuffle pushes the would-be usurper off and into the water. Fiesco's drowning cry is: "Genoa, help your Duke!" As Verrina announces that he will surrender to Andrea Doria, the curtain falls.

The first of the three ancillary plots has to do with Verrina and his family, and it patently depends both on Lessing's *Emilia Galotti* and on Lessing's own source in Livy's *History of Rome*. Verrina, returning home in the final scene of Act I, is confronted by his daughter Bertha, who informs him that she has been raped by Gianettino Doria. In fury the father recalls how, in Livy's *History*, Virginius slew his violated daughter Virginia. The girl is terrified. Just then arrive Verrina's friends Sacco and Calcagno and, presently, his prospective son-in-law Bourgognino. Verrina throws a veil over his daughter's head and vows she shall not again see the light of day until her ravisher has been slain. His three friends pledge their aid. In Act II these conspirators merge their plans with Fiesco's, but from the first moment Verrina divines Fiesco's real intentions. At the beginning of Act III, before Fiesco decides to make himself the next tyrant duke, Verrina takes young Bourgognino to the depths of a forest by night to whisper to him that Fiesco will have to be assassinated. These two appear in subsequent conspiracy scenes, but Bertha has only one brief moment more on stage, late in Act V. Her father has converted all his wealth into gold and put it on a ship, which he then instructs the young lovers to board at once and make their escape to Marseille.

In these two closely connected plots lies the gist of Schiller's political parable. Verrina, a grim old Puritan of a man, fiercely and unwaveringly believes in republican government. Fiesco, young, brilliant, sensual, and egotistical, uses the republican ideal only as a cover for his personal ambitions. Verrina—unhistorically—murders him, preferring the old tyrant to the new one, as long as the political ideal is unattainable anyway. Even without verbal hints in the text we could discern the parallels here with Brutus and Julius Caesar, both as those personages appear in classical sources and as they appear in Shakespeare's *Julius Caesar*. Schiller's own republicanism is, by the same token, shown as wistfully borrowed from Roman history of the first century B.C. From Shakespeare primarily are derived certain distinctions among the conspirators: Verrina and Brutus are motivated by political idealism; Sacco, like a shabbier Cassius, acts from need of money; Calcagno, vaguely like "the envious Casca," finds delight in sheer destruction.

A second ancillary plot concerns women characters, for, in contrast to the lone female role of Amalia in *The Robbers*, the present work has two prominent women's roles besides Bertha, as well as two small parts for ladies-in-waiting. Part of Fiesco's elaborate public deception consists of his heartless neglect of his wife Leonore. With reckless flamboyance he flirts with Gianettino's sister, the Countess Julia Doria, who very willingly flirts back. So distressing is all this to the sober young Bourgognino that he challenges Fiesco to a duel for Leonore's honor, but Fiesco neatly evades the challenge (Act I). In Act II Leonore discovers that her husband has apparently discarded her locket picture in favor of a locket picture of Julia Doria. Some tart words are exchanged between the two ladies over cups of hot chocolate at their next meeting.

The scene in Julia's apartments (III,3) is a dextrous game of betrayals and counterbetrayals, revelations and counterrevelations. Gianettino Doria, his suspicions of Fiesco aroused, has come to his sister to observe her as the barometer of passions in that liaison that seems to keep Fiesco—through Julia—faithfully in the Doria camp. Gianettino's questions irritate Julia, and she is still more irritated when the Doria henchman, Lomellin, intrudes into her quarters for a private talk with her brother. This is the point where she flounces over to the piano and dashes off "an Allegro" to vent her pique. Lomellin's fresh information is accurate and would be Fiesco's undoing if credited seriously. Just then Fiesco himself arrives and with dapper impudence allays suspicion of himself while coaxing Julia out of her bad humor. In Schiller's works we shall not again see the like of his maliciously and deliciously assisting her with her coiffure, her bosom covering, and her toilette, and persuading her to come out with him to entertainments, all the while parrying Gianettino's questions. When he escorts the lady out, the stupid Gianettino is smugly convinced that Fiesco is perfectly harmless.

A few hours before the uprising is due to begin, Fiesco's sorrowing wife Leonore, who has begged him for a separation, has followed his mysterious instructions to place herself behind a screen in the concert hall. There, together with her two ladies-in-waiting, Arabella and Rosa, she has a tedious wait. Then voices are heard, Fiesco enters in amorous converse with Julia. Wittily he leads her on to an open declaration of passion. When Julia has fallen to her knees with the cry of "I adore you, Fiesco!" he withdraws the screen to show her his beloved wife. Returning Julia her locket, that token of "a Harlequin passion," he brutally informs her that he is about to set out to murder her family. He points to his fellow conspirators, who have also been silent witnesses to every word. Julia flees, half hysterical, assuring Leonore that Fiesco will destroy her too—and himself. To his wife, Fiesco then says, "Go to bed, Countess. Tomorrow I shall waken—the Duchess." Leonore, already terrified, begs him to flee with her this very instant. He refuses, and the scene ends with the cannon shot that signals the moment of the uprising.

Amid the ensuing turmoil (Act V), Leonore seeks to flee, disguised as a man and accompanied by her faithful Arabella. The two are separated during the street fighting, and Leonore, rather implausibly, picks up the scarlet cloak that fell from the shoulders of the assassinated Gianettino and wraps it about her. In the darkness Fiesco mistakes her for his enemy and kills her, thus committing by accident the same action that Karl von Moor committed deliberately—the murder of his beloved, without whom life is worthless.

A third ancillary plot develops out of the deadly game of political chess played by the Dorias. Very near the beginning of the play, Gianettino Doria hired Muley Hassan, "a Moor from Tunis," to give Fiesco such a dagger thrust as would not leave him to suffer long. Before the end of Act I the Moor attempts to carry out this mission but is outwitted by Fiesco and ends up in Fiesco's service. From that point on, the

Moor is involved as the hero's agent at almost every turn of the story, bringing news, enlisting spies, controlling secret military operations, and carrying out moves to deceive the Dorias. In Act III, on Fiesco's instructions, he even lets himself be captured and put through the first degree of torture—before making a carefully prepared "confession." After all these efforts, Fiesco unexplainably dismisses him with contempt and with poor pay. Amid the street fighting in Act V Fiesco apprehends him in acts of wholesale arson and has him hanged.

Depending on one's conception of the play as a whole, Muley Hassan is either a dramatic nuisance or a show stealer. Certainly he is Schiller's most bizarre invention. On the cast-of-characters page the dramatist identifies him as "*ein konfiszierter Mohrenkopf*," his "physiognomy a unique mixture of rascality and humor." The first phrase lies somewhere between "a no-good Ayrab" and "a worthless infidel." The role requires a conscienceless cutthroat-for-hire who is quick-witted, resourceful, and physically brave. To submit himself to torture deliberately in his employer's interests is, to say the least, extraordinary. We are shocked that Fiesco should reward him so shabbily. The significant point about him, however, is that he is completely amoral, hence, from Schiller's point of view, abhorrent. Unfortunately, Fiesco also comes close to being amoral. In Act V the Moor's gratuitous acts of arson are unmotivated and our impression is that Schiller was determined to hang him. Quite literally his story ends with what the German language terms "gallows humor." If the Moor's role is taken as that of an exotic Till Eulenspiegel, the hanging is grotesque puppet-play stuff. Alternately, however, the role may be invested with a certain dignity, in which case it would be best if the Moor were allowed simply to disappear from the story after Act III, as his remote cousin, the dervish Al-Hafi, disappeared from Lessing's *Nathan the Wise*. Indeed, in the Mannheim premiere that is precisely what was done.

In the last analysis, *Fiesco* is not a historical drama of the kind Schiller was later to compose, but a costume play. As such we find it brilliant in spots, dull in others, and with an excess of plots. Our own taste would prefer the elimination of the Bertha story altogether; it is itself lugubrious and it comes off as a second-hand and second-best *Emilia Galotti*. We would further cut the text to concentrate on Fiesco himself, the women's roles, and Muley Hassan, while necessarily retaining the Doria characters. Then, with the understanding that no great profundity is at stake, we would recommend performing the work as unabashed melodrama amid a maximum of gorgeous color. The cast-of-characters page specifies that the Dorias wear scarlet, whereas Fiesco and all other nobles, including the ladies, wear black. If no color is indicated for Bertha, we suggest, without malice, that she be in white. In addition to these directions, many of the characters appear at the beginning of the play in masquerade-ball costumes.

The stage effects also merit special attention. Schiller had gained considerable insight into stage practices at the Mannheim Theater, and he exploited his new knowledge with enthusiasm in this play. The first four scenes of *Fiesco*, each a separate scene in the continental system of scene numbering, present encounters in what may be taken as a semiprivate palace room, but at the point where the continental system indicates Scene 5 and where we reckon no scene change, a midstage curtain is raised to prolong the spectators' view into the ballroom with its chandeliers and music and costumed guests. When the host is seeing his guests off, this "long stage" is made a "short stage" again by lowering the midstage curtain, so that the Moor's attempt to assassinate the hero is played forward, near the footlights. Meanwhile a crew of workmen is preparing "a room in Verrina's house," which will be revealed by opening the midstage curtain once more. By this simple device Schiller achieved a rapid and fluent procedure that he was to exploit with skill ever afterward.

Elaborate effects, familiar enough from operas, are also used in Act V. The spectators see first the city gate at stage rear, with the Mediterranean "in perspective" beyond it. After the striking colloquy where the hero talks from street level to Andrea Doria on the palace balcony, drums are heard on all sides, fighting is visible down by the city gate, and then suddenly the city gate is blown up spectacularly and the audience gains a wider view of the harbor full of lighted ships. The nearest ship, however, may have to be larger than perspective would normally require, because there, at stage rear, the hero must fall to his death.

The language of *Fiesco* improves on that of *The Robbers*. Speeches are shorter, on the whole. Monologues are much shorter. The cadences no more fall from an evangelical pulpit. Yet the styles are strangely mixed, as the actor Iffland mentioned at the time. The conspirators speak with Roman solemnity and sententiousness, the "social" scenes have a rococo sprightliness, the Moor has a humorous third style, while the distressed wife and her ladies talk in a style *larmoyant*. The surprising fact is that the rococo sprightliness comes off most successfully. It should also be mentioned that the text makes systematic use of animal imagery, chiefly of wild animals, probably in imitation of Shakespeare's *Coriolanus*.

We find this "Republican Tragedy" neither very

republican nor very tragic, and we prefer the conciliatory ending of the Mannheim premiere to Schiller's
"final version," with its forced and contrived deaths
that encumber his fifth act. We recognize the inven-
tive imagination that created this mood piece with its
sinister intrigue amid the opulence of masquerade, and
we remember it primarily as a movement of scarlet
and black masks in a nocturnal pageant of passion and
sudden death. Thus conceived and thus presented, it
could still provide a vivid evening in the theater.

Intrigue and Love

The title *Intrigue and Love* (*Kabale und Liebe*) was bestowed, at the actor Iffland's suggestion and at almost the last minute before publication on March 28, 1784, upon Schiller's third play, which he himself had thought of all along as "Luise Miller"; the subtitle, "a bourgeois tragedy," was, however, his own. The work was a great and immediate success in its two premieres—on April 13, by the Grossmann troupe in Frankfurt-am-Main, and on April 15, with a different cast, in Mannheim. In this latter, the star actor, Iffland, chose to play the role of Wurm and made much of the role. The very competent Becks, husband and wife, did well with the roles of Ferdinand and Luise. At the end of the second act the audience sprang to their feet and gave Schiller, in his loge, a standing ovation.

The time is the present, as of 1784. The place is an unnamed city, which any contemporary could have identified as Stuttgart. The tyrannical ruler of the unnamed principality is usually referred to as "the sovereign," but occasionally Schiller, intentionally or otherwise, calls him "the Duke." He never appears on stage, but his power is evident in the person of his prime minister, here called "President" von Walter.

Early in Act I, Mr. Wurm, secretary to the President, comes to call on his relative, the musician Miller. He is a red-haired, rat-faced sneak who expects to obtain Luise Miller in marriage by simply asking her father to give her to him. Miller bids the suitor sue directly to the girl, but Mrs. Miller, a hoity-toity social climber, signifies that Secretary Wurm does not stand a chance, because her daughter is destined for a noble marriage. Luise is indeed in love with Ferdinand von Walter, the President's son, and he with her, but between them are the barriers of social class. Her love is already half-paralyzed with fear of the President, but his love invokes God and the sublime laws of nature against any and all obstacles.

Before the curtain has risen on the second scene, Wurm has laid the facts before the President. The latter readily accords Luise to his secretary because, he says, his son will, beginning this very day, have more important things to do. The duke is about to take a duchess, hence, for appearances' sake, the duke's mistress, Lady Milford, must take a husband. The President's whole power depends on Lady Milford. Therefore, Ferdinand shall marry Lady Milford and keep the crucial influence "in the family." Just then the fatuous court fop, Chamberlain von Kalb, drops by for a chat and the President informs him of the forthcoming marriage of Ferdinand and Lady Milford, confident that anything known to Kalb will be known within an hour to the whole city. When he has left, Ferdinand arrives at his father's summons. The display of paternal tyranny that then ensues is such as never fails to rouse youthful readers and viewers to seething resentment; even middle-aged readers and viewers find it dismaying. Under dire threats Ferdinand promises to present himself at once to Lady Milford—but he will so effectively express his loathing of her that she will have no choice but to refuse him.

Lady Milford, as revealed in confidential talk with her maid Sophie in Act II, Scene 1, is a noble-hearted Englishwoman who has dedicated herself to the task of restraining the wanton excesses of her lover. Later, we learn how the duke rescued her, in despair and on the verge of suicide when family disasters had left her a penniless exile in Hamburg. What is more, she has long been in love with Ferdinand from afar.

Confirmation of her goodness follows immediately in a brief scene that is indeed memorable and which has always won American hearts for Schiller. An elderly valet brings her a casket of jewels as a gift from the duke. It transpires that the price of these jewels was met by the sale of seven thousand young men, by the head, to go as soldiers for England against the American Revolutionary Army. Among the cannon fodder are two sons of the old serving man himself. Lady Milford is aghast and immediately directs the resale of the jewels to help the needy.

Such roundups of young men were all too real a practice of the times. The Landgrave of Hesse-Cassel sold 17,000 men to England, the Duke of Brunswick 5,700, other German princes together another 8,000. If Charles Eugene of Württemberg sold no more than a battalion of men to England (as far as is known), he had sold many more than that to France and bloodily put down the mutinies of those who resisted. The money thus raised went for palace building, lavish entertainments, maintenance of mistresses, and displays of opulence while visiting other rulers.

In this brief scene, drama stops and nothing is heard but the voice of appalling truth declaring a crime against mankind. In barely two pages of text, Schiller says enough to warrant a revolution.

Inevitably, an audience is sobered and grim by the time Ferdinand is announced. The interview proceeds as neither he, nor the Lady, nor the audience had expected, and it ends in agreement by both parties to do their utmost to change the impossible situation in which they find themselves. Plot advancement and character revelation have been conducted simultaneously in a way that is nothing short of brilliant.

The Miller household is already in agitation as Act II, Scene 2 begins. An agent of the President has been making inquiries, and Miller sees at once that Wurm has taken his revenge for the snub he received. Miller proposes to go straight to the President, state the facts, and reach a frank agreement, but before he can set off, the arrival of Ferdinand increases everyone's terrors. Suddenly the President himself arrives with armed attendants. Brutally he questions Luise as a professional whore. Trying to shield her, Ferdinand defies his father. Mrs. Miller is in hysterics. Miller himself plucks up his courage and tells the President to get out. The President thunders that he will annihilate the Miller family. Beadles start to seize Luise from Ferdinand's very arms. Repeatedly Ferdinand fends them off with his sword, meanwhile addressing veiled threats to his father. Repeatedly the President orders the girl seized. All at once Ferdinand relinquishes the girl, shouting to his father that he will go immediately and tell everyone "the story of *how one gets to be President.*" For an instant the President does not believe his ears, then he shouts: "Let her go!"—as the curtain swiftly falls.

It was at this point that the premiere audience sprang to their feet and gave Schiller a standing ovation.

Unabashed melodrama it is, this II, 2, skillfully built up, masterfully reinforced by grotesque humor, and composed entirely of human elements—no moving saws, no speeding locomotives, or other gadgets associated with the term "melodrama." Only a heart of stone will fail to rouse to this excitement. Let us note also the objectivity of portrayal, with each character *in* character and with no editorializing by hero or dramatist.

From such a pitch it was wise to drop the opening of Act III down to a subdued tone. "The trick was ill-fated," the President is admitting to Wurm as the curtain rises; and Wurm replies: "As I feared, my Lord. Force always *embitters* fanatics, but never *converts* them." (The italics are part of Schiller's style.) Wurm now concocts a new stratagem, to which the President assents. The Millers shall be arrested; Luise shall be told their lives depend on her writing a certain letter, which Wurm will dictate to her; it will be a love letter to someone or other, and Ferdinand shall find it. Secrecy will be guaranteed by an oath—*those* people take oaths seriously. Along now comes Chamberlain von Kalb, who is talked into acting as the necessary someone with whom Luise is in love.

In a carefully built-up atmosphere of uncertainty and dread, III, 2 proceeds from a near quarrel between Ferdinand and Luise to the scene of Wurm's dictation of the love letter.

A deceived and raging Ferdinand confronts the preposterous Kalb in IV, 1, insisting on a duel to the death, until the terrified little man confesses the truth as far as he knows it. Ferdinand dismisses him with contempt, but still believes Luise to be false. Act IV, Scene 2 brings Luise to Lady Milford at the latter's summons. The feline antipathies displayed by these two "good" characters have puzzled many people, but Schiller doubtless understood that such was the predictable conduct of rival females. The act ends with Luise's renunciation of Ferdinand and with Lady Milford's asking Chamberlain von Kalb to deliver to the duke an insulting letter of farewell from his mistress.

The long Act V, in one continuous scene, dwells on

the grief and terror of Luise and her father and on
Ferdinand's love-hate ambivalence as the three of them
meet in Miller's house. (Unaccountably, Mrs. Miller
disappears from the story after Act II.) Ferdinand,
deciding to "crush the adder before she stings her father too," has Luise prepare a glass of lemonade, into
which he surreptitiously pours poison. Miller is sent
off with a message to the President. Gloomily Ferdinand persuades Luise to share the poisoned drink with
him, prolonging his ironic conversation with her until
she realizes that she has come to the last hour of her
life. The fact releases her from her sacramental oath,
and she tells the truth about the letter and the whole
deception. The President arrives in great perturbation
at his son's message; Wurm and officers are with him.
Then truths are declared on all sides, the father plead-
ing for his son's forgiveness and denouncing Wurm as
the sole cause of all their misfortunes. Wurm sneers at
this denunciation and vows to reveal the President's
secrets to the authorities. Ferdinand, no longer capable
of speech, extends his dying hand to his father in sign
of forgiveness. The President with great joy cries out:
"He forgave me!" then turns to the officers and says:
"Now: your prisoner!" as the curtain falls.

Character Prototypes

Most of what Schiller said or implied about his offstage duke was true of Charles Eugene of Württemberg, whose long reign from 1744 to 1793 was based
on the principles of taxation, confiscation, and imprisonment. He scoffed at the two-centuries-old constitu-
tion of the duchy and said: *"Ich bin das Vaterland,"*
either inventing the phrase or recalling Louis XIV's
alleged remark: *"L'état, c'est moi!"* He lived scandal-

:ce 1784

When, in June of 1784, Schiller addressed the ·annheim German Society, he declared his intention · using drama as an instrument for trying social cul-·its before the court of public opinion. Ironically, he ·as soon to arrive at the notion that such use of drama ·as wholly improper. Ten years later, in 1794, when ·Joethe requested him to update *Intrigue and Love* for ·he Weimar stage, he not only declined to do so but, ·s long as he lived, he refused to allow the work to be performed there.

Meanwhile the play was being performed in almost every theater in Protestant Germany—even in Stuttgart! But there certain nobles protested that it was offensive and Duke Charles Eugene banned it. Reviews were full of praise, yet, among them, they singled out every weakness that common sense could discover in the plot, and several of them deplored the (deplorable) bombast with which the characters speak. Nevertheless, the play's popularity irresistibly increased, both in German-speaking lands and in translations into almost every European language. New York saw the English adaptation on May 10, 1799, under Monk Lewis's title of *The Minister*, and on December 13, 1813, Philadelphia saw the same version under the new title of *The Harper's Daughter, or Love and Ambition.*

In 1854, when a Munich theater staged twelve revivals from Lessing, Goethe, and Schiller, *Intrigue and Love* was accorded two performances out of the twelve, as box-office insurance. Between 1870 and 1889, Theodor Fontane, as drama reviewer, had occasion to write about twenty different stagings of the work. In 1905, the centenary of Schiller's death, this play still outranked all other works by Schiller except

ously in reckless extravagance. Displays of fireworks, such as Lady Milford mentions early in Act II, might consume "½ ton of gold" in a few minutes.

Lady Milford is a tolerably accurate portrayal of Charles Eugene's mistress, Franziska von Hohenheim, save that her British origins and her penniless exile in Hamburg are Schiller's inventions. When she was twenty-one and had already endured five years of marriage to the surly Baron von Leutrum, Charles Eugene began pursuing her, not for her beauty, for she was rather plain, but for her character. Two years later, in 1771, she fled to her ducal lover. A divorce was obtained for the Leutrums in 1772; in 1774 Franziska became Countess of Hohenheim by order of the emperor; in 1785, when the legitimate but absent duchess died, Charles Eugene married his dear "Franzele." Never did he permit her, however, to interfere in matters of state, nor did she herself aspire to do so. In her sincere love for him she was often able to moderate his excesses, and the people of the duchy understood and revered her benevolence. For her birthday in 1779, the twenty-year-old Schiller delivered a school eulogy in her honor.

The President and Wurm are also derived from actual persons, the former from Count Samuel Friedrich von Montmartin, the latter from Montmartin's accomplice, one Lorenz Wittleder, an ex-journeyman-tanner and a seller of public offices. In 1762 they contrived to oust Charles Eugene's prime minister, Philipp Friedrich Rieger, on trumped-up charges of treason, and sent him, without a hearing, to Hohentwiel dungeon to languish for four years amid filth and semistarvation. Abruptly, in 1766, and without any explanations they were dismissed from service and Rieger was brought back from prison and reinstated in office. Thus "the story of how one gets to be President" was no idle jest, while the surrender of the two villains at the end of our play had a real-life counterpart, considerably more grim but too complex to account for in the drama scenario.

Of the ten persons who enact our play, not counting the offstage duke, history vouches for three: the President (Montmartin), Wurm (Lorenz Wittleder), and Lady Milford (Franziska von Hohenheim). Hence the work is, to some degree, a documentary. Lady Milford's maid Sophie represents the stock type of the confidante from both traditional tragedy and traditional comedy, while Chamberlain von Kalb is a variation of a stock buffoon from comedy tradition, particularly in his exaggerations of French courtly elegance. The nameless valet who speaks with "the voice of the people" appears in only one brief scene. Ferdinand and the three members of the Miller family are wholly fictional and derive, in differing degrees, from Lessing's *Emilia Galotti* of 1772, a scant dozen years before.

The Millers, mother and father, live perceptibly lower on the social scale than the Galottis, so that where Claudia was only somewhat foolishly sentimental in regard to her daughter, Mrs. Miller is downright fatuous, and where Odoardo was the strong and dignified head of a household, Miller, while loyal-hearted enough, often ineffectually blusters. His crudities of language and his wife's malapropisms had no counterpart in Lessing's play. Luise and Emilia are equally pious, dutiful, and virtuous, but Luise is wholly without blemish, whereas Lessing's heroine had her interesting secret impulse to illicit love, that trait that caused Goethe to raise an eyebrow and that disciples of Freud are tickled to discover. The problem of class barriers is wholly Schiller's; Emilia Galotti was happily betrothed to Count Appiani until the self-indulgent prince yielded to his vicious secretary,

Marinelli, in the plot to waylay th and kidnap the bride. Even the str *and Love* parallels the structure of both follow the pattern of stratag stratagem–disaster—so that it is con Schiller composed his drama "with open on the table beside him."

The essential change made by Schill whereby the action is made to depend tion of social classes. His offstage duke a President are aristocrats corrupted bey tion, and his bourgeois Wurm is corrupt cratic association, while the bourgeois wholly guiltless. In this point lies the "rev quality of the play. Moreover, the goodl bourgeois characters lies in their capacity affections, for feeling, whereas the wickedn aristocrats lies in their heartlessness. Here is for Dostoevsky's future division, in *The Inst Injured* of 1861, of human beings into the tv gories of "Schillers" (or lambs) and "wolves."

Ferdinand, as a good aristocrat, is the excep the rule. He is a problematical hero, closely a Karl von Moor and to Fiesco. In different degre in different combinations, all three are melanchol aloof, precipitate to action, and given to a ce authoritarian willfulness. All three slay the wo they love, and if Ferdinand shares the poison v Luise, he morbidly indulges himself in watching slow death. The implied question of all three heroes Would you die for me? But, as if they dreaded th answer to be no, they determine the outcome them selves, until the dramatist seems to be advocating literary form of suttee. This fact is all the more puz zling since in these years Schiller had neither wife nor sweetheart.

for the phenomenally popular *William Tell.* By 1895 the text of *Intrigue and Love* had been edited for use in German schools. The American school edition, with more than a hundred pages of introductory matter and more than a hundred pages of textual notes by W. A. Hervey of Columbia University, appeared in 1912. From 1784 until approximately 1920, the play commanded international admiration almost to idolatry.

Around 1920, however, it suffered a decline, and since 1950 it has had hard going. For a 1963 festival production much of Act IV was cut, intrigue was reduced to a minimum, and love was given a wider scope. Helmut Griem, as Ferdinand, made the role a study of an overintense and morbidly jealous lover of a quiet but intense Luise. The Millers were coarsened and the President was interpreted as a coolly calculating man.

The Munich production of 1965 reduced the Millers to slum dwellers and showed the aristocrats as uncouth decadents swilling and spilling their alcoholic beverages amid settings of garish bad taste. The bald and jovial President, razor-witted under fat, accepted the familiarities of a Wurm who was a hapless little failure of a man. The Bremen performance of 1967, on the other hand, cut much of Ferdinand's role to concentrate on the sweet sadness of a wrecked love.

It is questionable whether Schiller would have been gratified by these specialized and forced interpretations of his play. Before the end of the 1780s he had himself outgrown *Intrigue and Love* and its predecessor plays and would have liked to disavow all three of them. In his poet's Elysium he may, around 1920, have concluded that a hundred and forty years of uninterrupted successes were enough for this work. Our own feeling is that *Intrigue and Love* is now a venerable museum piece.

Don Carlos

Confidently and with no anticipation of any difficulties, Schiller began making sketches for his fourth play, *Don Carlos*, in March, 1783, immediately after completing the draft of *Intrigue and Love* and before extensive revisions of that work took him away from his new creation. By December a completed Act I of *Don Carlos*, in prose, was given a public reading in Darmstadt in the presence of Duke Charles Augustus of Weimar, and that same Act I, in prose, was later published in March, 1785, in the first—and only—issue of Schiller's literary magazine *The Rhenish Thalia*. Subsequently, his successor magazine, *The Thalia*, carried installments of the work in progress up as far as the end of III, 2 (III, 9 in the continental system of scene numbering) and to what was later to be line 2940 of the blank-verse text. This prose version was eventually completed and even used in performance, but midway through the struggle with his artistic material, Schiller recast his prose as blank verse and went on to complete his drama in terms very different from what he had originally planned.

What ultimately emerged in June, 1787, as *Don Carlos: A Dramatic Poem* was a work running to

6,282 lines. For the 1801 edition of the play this text was reduced to 5,448 lines, and just prior to his death in 1805 Schiller established a definitive text of 5,370 lines. The uncharacteristic delays in composition betoken the supreme artistic crisis of Schiller's life, and the artistic crisis in turn betokens a major psychological crisis. What he had begun was a fourth play in his storm-and-stress manner, and up to line 2940 of the finished product we have essentially just that. What he composed from line 2940 on struggles at times to reconcile the already published first half with the new dramatic ideas, but it emerges, particularly in Act V, as the work of a very great dramatist. The finished product, even at 5,370 lines, is excessively long and it is not precisely in focus, but the second half attains such rare heights that we reckon the total play among Schiller's masterpieces.

Sources and History

As undertaken in the spring of 1783, *"Dom" Carlos* was to have been a dramatization, with appropriate modifications, of the once-popular French prose romance of 1672, *Dom Carlos, Nouvelle Historique*, by the Abbé César Vichard de Saint-Réal. That eighty-page tale proclaims itself at the outset a true narration of the historical facts concerning Don Carlos, crown prince of Spain, who died in 1568, and it is footnoted with references to "manuscripts as well as printed works" from "all the Spanish, French, Italian, and Flemish authors who have written about the era." Yet there is hardly a word of historical truth in it.

It opens with the prince's arrival at the French border to escort his betrothed, the French Princess Elizabeth de Valois, home to Madrid and marriage—to his father. Diplomats, it seems, have changed their minds: not the son, as first planned, but the father and reigning king must be the bridegroom in this union of political advantage. Not a word of this is true.

Once the May-December wedding has taken place, according to Saint-Réal, the gray-haired King Philip II is tormented with jealous suspicions about his young wife. His own half brother, Don Juan of Austria, does fall in love with his new sister-in-law, but his adulterous suit is rejected. Likewise rejected are the amatory designs upon the king himself by the "irregularly" beautiful Princess of Eboli, but, nothing daunted, that lady redirects her designs upon Don Carlos, where she is rejected anew. These two thwarted persons then contrive together to ruin both the young queen and the prince. The jealous king himself, meanwhile suspects now his son and now his son's friend, the Marquis of Posa, of being the queen's secret lover. Deciding at last that his son must be the guilty party, he orders his arrest, finds incriminating letters to confirm his suspicions, and turns the letters over to the Inquisition. The doomed Carlos is allowed an easy suicide by opening his veins in a hot bath. Hurried concluding statements add that Spanish historians have falsified these "facts" to flatter the tyrannical king and that the incriminating letters were later shown to be forgeries by the Princess of Eboli.

From March, 1783, there are preserved a few pages of terse memoranda, known as "The Bauerbach Sketch," to show some of Schiller's first intentions for his drama. Don Juan of Austria is omitted altogether. The note to the effect that "the Marquis" diverts suspicion to himself suggests that Posa's self-sacrifice for his friend was Schiller's new plot ingredient from the outset. The scenario must also have planned a different ending from what we know, because another note says: "The testimony of the dying woman . . . justifies the Prince too late."

Belatedly, in 1785, Schiller learned that this history was no history at all. The actual Don Carlos was a subnormal youth who was imprisoned by his father and grimly allowed to die because he was unthinkable as future ruler of the most powerful kingdom in the world. From the Venetian ambassador's report to his home government we learn that Carlos, at age thirteen, was haughty, brutal, intolerable; that he practiced loathsome cruelty on animals, such as roasting a rabbit alive; that he was already a skirt chaser and a spendthrift. A second Venetian ambassador described Carlos at age eighteen (1563) as undersized, ugly, physically weak, dull in studies as in athletics, ill-tempered, vicious, and vindictive. The French ambassador's report to Paris even spoke of *imbécilité*.

During the Christmas season of 1567, King Philip retired to ascetic seclusion in his somber rural palace of the Escorial and from there ordered prayers to be said beginning January 12, 1568, for his divine guidance in serious decisions. Returning to Madrid on January 17, he solemnly consigned his son to close guard in a palace room, and there the twenty-three-year-old prince languished, alternately fasting and gorging himself, until he died of natural causes six months later.

The subnormal son was his father's grief and shame, and Philip did everything possible to conceal the ugly details from the public. From that secrecy rumors and speculations inevitably grew, especially in hostile Protestant lands. Over the years a legend of Don Carlos slowly formed, and we can describe this legend as the consolidated Protestant gossip about Don Carlos: he was a splendid youth, inclined to religious toleration and to independence for the Spanish Neth-

erlands, and for these reasons he was betrayed by the
Princess of Eboli and slain by the Inquisition, though
the actual charge was his love for his young stepmother, to whom he had been originally betrothed.
Elements of this legend can be traced to different persons at different times, but in its general outlines it was
commonly accepted as historical truth in Protestant
lands and in France by, let us say, 1668, the centenary
of the real Carlos's death. All the Abbé de Saint-Réal
had to do in 1672 was to write it out in entertaining
prose.

Discovering all this when his drama was half-
written must have been most disconcerting to Schiller.
Worse still, the historical facts were of no use to him.
He could not adjust his plans to accommodate them,
and a drama based on the actual Carlos would not suit
his purposes at all. There was nothing to do but continue with his scenario as it was. And that is what he
did.

The Play as far as Line 2940

It is eight months since the suspicious king has recalled his son from the university of Alcalá in order to
keep him under surveillance, and still the young man
remains withdrawn in unexplained melancholy. The
priest Domingo, as one of Philip's spies, is badgering
the prince as the play opens. With ironic and elusive
replies Carlos gets rid of him. Just then arrives Rode-
rick, Marquis of Posa, a boyhood friend just returned
from the Low Countries, where Spanish oppression of
Protestants is causing havoc. The two friends pledge
eternal devotion to one another and to the ideal of
religious toleration. Carlos then confesses that he is in
love with the queen, just as his father suspects, and

begs Posa to help him to a private interview with his "mother." Posa agrees to do so.

By withdrawing the midstage curtain, Act I, Scene 1, which took place in a section of the royal garden at Aranjuez, opens up into a larger prospect of the garden, where I, 2 discovers the queen among her ladies. She asks to see her young daughter, but rigid Spanish etiquette forbids that until a prescribed hour. Posa is announced. Cleverly he engages and disengages attention until he is able to bring Carlos before the queen when all her ladies are dispersed about the garden. For her stepson, the queen disallows all save a maternal love, but she listens with sympathy to the tale of distress in the Low Countries. Hardly has Carlos withdrawn when the king appears with a retinue of gentlemen, and, to his anger, finds his royal spouse unattended. The Marquise of Mondecar, quickly appearing, has barely begun to apologize for this breach in court etiquette when Philip banishes her from Madrid for ten years. The queen dismisses Mondecar with regret and with a gift, saying, "In my France it was otherwise." When the king inquires about his son, there is silence. The Duke of Alba assures Philip he need fear no one, while the old Count of Lerma warmly defends Carlos.

By closing the midstage curtain, I, 3 is played on the narrow forestage. There Posa informs Carlos that the Duke of Alba has been appointed governor of the Low Countries—the worst possible man for the post. Carlos, knowing now that the queen is sympathetic to the cause of toleration, declares he will obtain an audience with his father the next day and beg to be appointed in Alba's stead. The act closes with still stronger affirmations of brotherhood between Carlos and Posa.

In II, 1 Carlos pleads his case to his father, and when

his father refuses, he throws himself totally upon his father's mercy, saying that Madrid oppresses him and that he desperately needs a change of scene. With aversion the king refuses that request too, yet when his son is gone, he speaks somewhat caustically to the Duke of Alba: perhaps he has listened too one-sidedly to Alba's insinuated suspicions; at any rate Carlos shall stand nearer to the throne—at least for a period of trial.

Near the door of the queen's apartments (II, 2), a page hands Carlos an unsigned love-assignation note. Out from the queen's apartments comes the Duke of Alba, with whom Carlos gets into an altercation. Just as swords are drawn, the queen emerges to utter the single word of reproof: "Carlos!" Immediately Carlos puts up his sword, asks pardon of Alba, suddenly kisses him, and swiftly leaves.

Eagerly following the instructions in the unsigned note, Carlos comes in II, 3 to an apartment where he fully expects to see the queen. Instead, he finds the Princess of Eboli. In his bewilderment he says just enough to allow Eboli to deduce who it was that he expected to find, but she in turn produces a letter from the king asking her to become the royal mistress. When the scene ends, each party is in possession of dangerous secrets of the other, Carlos by keeping his father's love letter, Eboli by thinking through, in a final monologue, the fragments of evidence before her.

In II, 4 the two spies, Domingo and the Duke of Alba, pool their own evidence and suspicions. Their objective is to destroy both Carlos and the queen as potentially dangerous liberals. Domingo, as go-between for Eboli and the king, suggests that Eboli may be induced to abet their schemes. In fact, he is waiting for her right now. Along she comes, in an outrage of hurt pride at Carlos's rejection and jealous of the queen as a successful rival. She agrees to become the king's mistress and to follow Domingo's hint that the queen's private correspondence can be purloined: very likely some incriminating letters from or to the prince will be found.

Act II, Scene 5 brings Carlos and Posa to a secret rendezvous at a Carthusian monastery. Carlos wants a second interview with the queen in order to show her his father's self-incriminating letter to Eboli, but Posa tears the letter up. Posa sees, as Carlos does not, that Eboli is a jealous woman in possession of mortally dangerous information. He however, has a new idea of great importance, not to be disclosed now, but perhaps Carlos will learn of it from the queen herself no later than tomorrow.

Scenes 1, 3, and 5 of Act II have been played on the "long stage," while Scenes 2 and 4 have been played on the shallow forestage. The former used sets for the king's audience room, Eboli's apartment, and the monastery, while the latter used almost no sets or stage properties for the encounter before the queen's door or for the conference of the three spies.

In the long III, 1, the king is discovered near dawn in his bedchamber after a sleepless night. Before his staring eyes lie on a table the pieces of evidence obtained by Eboli: a medallion portrait of Carlos and some letters. To the Count of Lerma, who guards the royal door, he addresses wild words about husbands who trust their wives. To Alba, whom he has summoned at this unwonted hour, the king shows the evidence, only to have Alba goad his suspicions still further. Domingo, summoned in turn, even insinuates that the little Princess Clara Eugenia is not Philip's child. So monstrous do these insinuations seem to the king that he doubts everything the two schemers have proposed and he dismisses them angrily. At line 2809, he speaks a kind of prayer, beginning, "Good Providence, give me a human being," and he goes on to express his anguished need of one true friend whom he can trust. He leafs through a memorandum book and comes upon the name of the Marquis of Posa, underlined with double bar and with notations of praise beside it in the margin. He cannot recall who this Posa is, but perhaps he is the "human being" he so desperately needs.

In his audience that morning (III, 2), he makes inquiry about this Marquis of Posa and hears glowing reports of him, even from Alba. He bids Alba bring Posa to him in the royal study after Mass.

This scene ends at line 2940.

Shift of Viewpoints; Hamlet

Thus far, *Don Carlos* is a family tragedy. A husband, himself disloyal, is tormented with jealousy of his young wife. Mutual antipathy divides father from son. The son and his young stepmother love each other, but adulterous passion exists—unfulfilled—only in the son's heart. Eboli, an outsider, has sought the son's love, but, in rejection, she accepts the father's adulterous proposal, the better to revenge herself on her rejecter and on her rival. Domingo and Alba are gratuitous mischief-makers. Posa is Carlos's loyal friend, but his dramatic function is that of a benign confidant and go-between.

Beginning with III, 3 (in the German, III, 10), this straightforward analysis will no longer be valid. What we term "the poetic center of gravity" will be shifted, because Schiller came to see his story from a different perspective, and as a result the play is, so to speak, slightly out of focus. Scenes, especially in Act IV, will seek to reconcile the two dramatic viewpoints, without full success. Yet, oddly enough, out of the awkwardness will emerge "the greater half" of the play.

Distinct, probably, from the shifting of viewpoints was a separate process by which Schiller came to see his scenario "through the prism" of Shakespeare's *Hamlet*. Don Carlos and Hamlet—each is a crown prince returned from school to live in a home court riddled with intrigue and in the shadow of a king who dislikes him and distrusts him. The mother of each, for different reasons, is ambiguous in her maternal affections. Each royal father despises his "weakling" heir but admires an energetic and unproblematical young man of the court, and each sets a team of spies to report every word and deed of the hero's. The parallels extend to the Count of Lerma and Polonius, to Don Luis Mercado and Osric, and even to the rumor of Emperor Charles V's ghost and the actual ghost of Hamlet's father. Schiller's shift of viewpoint is betokened by the fact that before III, 3 Posa stands parallel to Horatio, and after that point combines the dramatic functions of Horatio and Laertes. The scenario, meanwhile, remains unchanged; but the dramatist now sees Saint-Réal's characters as having the dramatic values of the characters in *Hamlet*, with the result that his play gains a marked intensity.

Don Carlos, *III, 3*

The most famous, but not the greatest, scene in the play is III, 3, the king's interview with Posa in the royal study. Impressed alike by the young man and his record, the king inquires why he has resigned from royal service. Posa's circumspect answer leads up to the famous line: "I cannot be the server of a Prince"— a line which he repeats after further statement. For a

moment the king suspects him of crypto-Protestant-
ism, but Posa assures him they share one faith. Discussion of philosophy, however, leads Posa on to ardent
declarations of belief that are entirely of Schiller's
epoch and quite literally unthinkable in 1568. In his
ardor he mentions the oppression recently witnessed
in the Low Countries. The king replies that he means
to give those provinces the same cloudless peace en-
joyed in Spain. "The peace of cemeteries!" cries Posa,
and he implores the king to see the difference between
monarchs who rule over human beings and those who
destroy life. He begs him:

> "Walk at the head of all the kings of Europe.
> A single pen-stroke will suffice: the world
> Will be created new. O give us freedom
> Of thought . . ."

"Fantastic visionary!" interrupts the king, but he listens further, cautioning Posa eventually: "But avoid
my Inquisition." Inspired by this youth of noble and
independent ideas, Philip at last confesses the bitter
troubles of his family life and points to the evidence
lying on the table. Half in plea, half in command, he
says:

> "Make your way to my son's favor,
> And sound the Queen's heart out. I will send you
> Full authorization to speak with them both
> In private."

When Posa has left, the king instructs the Count of
Lerma, keeper of the door:

> "The cavalier
> Will henceforth be admitted unannounced."

Act IV

Of the eight scenes of Act IV, a total of 1,133 lines, only Scene 5 (66 lines) is nonessential. We summarize as follows:

1. Using his new authority, Posa goes to the queen to propose that Carlos should escape to the Low Countries at once. The queen agrees and so signifies in a hasty note to Carlos.

2. Lerma worriedly reports to Carlos that Posa was two hours with the king in secret talk, of which he heard only snatches where the queen was mentioned. He hints that Posa may be betraying Carlos, but Carlos dismisses the idea. Along comes Posa, unaware of what Lerma has said, and answers his friend's questions with airy evasions. He delivers the queen's note, then asks for Carlos's letter case with all its contents, including a treasured letter from the queen when Carlos was ill in Alcalá. Carlos complies, but begins to believe that Posa is one of his father's spies.

3. The queen asks her husband to find the thief who rifled her jewel casket, taking jewels, letters, and a medallion portrait of Carlos. This last is found on the floor by their three-year-old daughter, who brings it to her mother. In the ensuing altercation the king blurts out the word "adultress" and even thrusts the child away from his wife. With the child snatched up in her embrace, the queen collapses in a faint at the door. Alba and Domingo, hovering near, rush in, only to be savagely denounced as traitors. Posa arrives. He hands the king Carlos's letter case, which now contains only innocent papers and Eboli's unsigned love assignation. The king recognizes Eboli's handwriting, guesses at her alliance with Alba and Domingo, and yields himself wholly to Posa's trust. Posa requests and

obtains from him a written order for Carlos's arrest. (He intends protective custody.)

4. Lerma warns Carlos anew, relating how he saw Posa hand the king Carlos's letter case. Carlos is now convinced Posa is his enemy and rushes off to his one remaining friend. (In IV, 6 we learn that this friend is Eboli.)

5. Alba and Domingo warn the queen that Posa is her enemy, perhaps even the thief of her jewel casket, but the queen indignantly rejects their guile.

6. Carlos begs Eboli's pardon for his previous unkindness and implores of her one favor: to arrange for him to speak with his "mother." In rushes Posa with officers and arrests Carlos before he can speak any further self-incriminating word. Then, placing her dagger point, he tries to force Eboli to disclose what Carlos has said to her. Suddenly, with the words "There is another way," he releases Eboli and rushes away. (The other way will be diversion of suspicion from Carlos by incriminating himself.)

7. Eboli, distraught with terror and remorse, reports Posa's arrest of Carlos to the queen. Because Posa made the arrest, the queen is unperturbed, but Eboli is sure Carlos faces execution for treason. She confesses rifling the jewel casket—for love of Carlos. The queen instantly pardons her: anything is pardonable for love of Carlos. But Eboli goes on to confess her adultery with the king, whereupon the queen walks away, sending the Duchess of Olivarez to announce Eboli's sentence to a cloister. Suddenly Eboli rushes away. (We learn later that she means to confess everything to the king.) Posa comes to the queen for a last farewell, hinting that his death is imminent. Carlos, he says, is safe but should escape this very night; the queen is to tell him that Posa was true to him and that the new golden age must wait until Carlos becomes king. With

the cry: "My God, but life is beautiful," he leaves her.

8. Outside the king's door the nobles are in excitement: Carlos is imprisoned and the royal postmaster has intercepted a letter of Posa's to the rebels in the Low Countries. (We learn later that in the letter Posa declared himself the queen's secret lover and showed all his actions, including his friendship with the king, to be devices of deception.) No one is allowed in to see the king, but presently Lerma emerges from the royal study with the flabbergasting news that the king —is weeping! Eboli comes rushing in on her last errand of desperation, but she is not allowed to see the king. At last Alba is summoned; he comes back out triumphant, bidding Domingo have *Te Deum* sung in all the churches, for "the victory is ours!"

Act V

From the foregoing complexities the three scenes of the final act rise to grandeur. To Carlos's prison room comes Posa for a last farewell. Their long conversation is interrupted once by Alba, who comes in the king's name to restore Carlos's sword. Proudly Carlos retorts that he will accept it only from the king himself.

Between the friends everything is made clear. All of Posa's actions, including the arrest of his friend, were intended to prevent him from self-incriminations with anyone, most of all with Eboli—of whose genuine remorse Posa is unaware. Such is Carlos's love for his friend that he meekly bore the supposed betrayal; he even suggests that Posa, as the king's advisor, may achieve the golden age that he himself might have bungled.

The entire tragedy, we now infer, has resulted from a double flaw in an otherwise perfect trust: Carlos's doubt of Posa's loyalty and Posa's well-meant evasion of Carlos's questions—he intended to tell Carlos only when success had been achieved. The "guiltless guilt" lies with Lerma. By a pitiful coincidence, Lerma saw and overheard either too little or too much. Here, then, is a tragic drama wholly independent of Aristotle's conceptions.

When Posa has at last made clear the decoy letter, which must now be in the king's hands, Carlos is horrified. He will reveal the deception and rescue Posa, but the latter bids him preserve himself for the sake of the Low Countries' cause. No, says Carlos, they will go together to the king, explain everything, and the king will be moved to forgiveness when he hears that "A friend has done this for his friend." At that instant a shot is fired and Posa is killed. With a cry, Carlos drops to the floor beside him and remains so, unaware that around him have gathered the king and a retinue of nobles.

Dazed with grief, Carlos lets himself be drawn to his feet and into his father's arms, but, as he becomes aware, he wrenches himself free with the cry: "The smell of you is murder." Indignantly the king starts to leave, but Carlos, with the sword the king has just brought him, forces him to listen.

When Philip read Posa's decoy letter (IV, 8), he had wept, wept for affection and trust wasted on a traitor. For Philip, the tears were, in themselves, a monstrous experience, but they were shed in private and for a private betrayal of a kind that rulers may expect. Now he must publicly hear far worse betrayal. Savagely Carlos explains that Posa duped the king for the sake of a greater friendship:

"His noble life was love. And love for me
Was his great noble death. And he was *mine*
While you were touting his respect for you ...

     .   .   .

"You fancied you had mastered him—and were
The docile instrument of his high plans.

     .   .   .

    "You may have accorded him
Your favor—but he died for me. Your heart
And friendship you had forced upon him, but
Your scepter was the plaything of his hands;
He threw it down and died for me!"

For sixty-eight lines Carlos continues his hysterical
taunts, bidding his father go find himself a son among
strangers, until, with the cry of "Here lie my kingdoms!" he sinks down beside the corpse of Posa and
totally disregards what ensues. At this shattering moment one-half of the stage contains the corpse of Posa
with Carlos clinging to it, wide emptiness around the
two, while the other half of the stage contains the king
with a cluster of awed, almost frightened, noblemen
around him. The king has listened to Carlos's invective
—perforce, but he is wrought to a frightful pitch.
From his shoulders he tears off the royal mantle and
throws it upon the unnoticing Carlos—and then collapses in a faint.

Behind the figures of Philip, Posa, and Carlos loom
up at this moment not the Shakespearean figures of
King Claudius, Laertes, and Hamlet previously mentioned, but a trio of characters mightier still: Saul,
David, and Jonathan, as of I Samuel 18:1–20:42 and of
II Samuel 1:17–27. (Lines 5250–51 will presently
allude to another portion of I Samuel.)

The grandees carry King Philip away. The silent
stage is empty, save for Posa's corpse and Carlos clinging to it, lost in grief. Then comes Don Luis Mercado

with a message to Carlos from the queen. Even the queen's name elicits from Carlos only the reply: "Nothing in this world is of importance to me now," but as soon as the messenger speaks the name of Posa, Carlos springs to his feet, all attention. The queen bids him come to her at midnight garbed as a monk; if he is seen, people will assume it is the ghost of Emperor Charles V, Carlos's grandfather, who is said to haunt the palace in monk's garb. (The real Charles V abdicated his throne in 1556 and retired to a monastery, where he died in 1558; our play is set in 1568.)

Hardly has the messenger departed when the Count of Lerma comes to Carlos with a further message from the queen: he must flee to the Low Countries this very day. Hailing Carlos as "my children's king," Lerma guides him away, but not before Carlos has once more embraced the corpse of Posa.

In V, 2, Alba is again at the king's door, where no one is being admitted. His urgent news is that a certain monk has been arrested, a monk from the Carthusian monastery where Carlos and Posa used to meet in secret, and on the monk's person have been found letters from Posa to Carlos outlining a detailed plot for the liberation of the Low Countries from Spain by force. Suddenly the king emerges from his study, his garments awry, his looks wild, and speaking as though to unseen persons in total disregard for the persons actually present. Harshly he rebuffs Alba, then continues with his own obsessive thoughts:

> "He had a friend who died for him—for him!
> With me he could have shared a royal kingdom!
> How he looked down on me!"

Through more than forty lines the king writhes in mental agony over his own love rejected and over his detested son as the recipient of the love that he, the king, so desperately craved and that he had believed was his.

> "He did not sacrifice his Philip for
> His Carlos, but the old man for the young
> One, his disciple; for the father's sunset
> No longer makes the day's work worth the effort."

But this partial rationalization will not suffice. Indeed, there is no rationalization. And now, at line 5075, the intensity of love passes over into hate even as we watch. He will use "the evening of his life" to wreak such revenge that for

> "Ten human ages after me no sower
> Shall reap again this charred and fire-swept field.
> He sacrificed me to humanity,
> His idol: let humanity atone
> For him!"

Philip is now the fallen Lucifer in the pit of hell, vowing destruction on the heaven of love.

A guard enters with the report that the ghost of Charles V, clad as a monk, has been seen passing through corridors and disappearing into the queen's apartments. Philip orders that wing of the palace cordoned off.

At this point it would seem that the drama had reached the limits of emotion and power, but Schiller now presents a stupendous *plus ultra*. The king dismisses all attendants to be alone with his Grand Inquisitor, whom he has summoned.

"Enter the Cardinal Grand Inquisitor, ninety years of age and blind, leaning on a staff, and led by two Dominicans."

To him the gray-haired king is a willful and errant boy. Everything about this dangerous man Posa, he tells the king, has long been known; and when the astonished king asks why he was not so informed, the Inquisitor blames him for not inquiring and bitterly denounces him for having Posa shot:

> "Who authorized *you* to lay hands
> Upon the Order's sacred property?
> To die for us was his excuse for living.
> God granted him unto this epoch's need
> To make of swaggering Reason an example
> By formal degradation of his mind.
>
> .   .   .
>
> "We have been cheated, robbed, and you have
>   nothing
> But bloody hands."

For the king's excuses: "My passion swept me on," "I looked into his eyes," "I yearned for just one human being," the Inquisitor has nothing but contempt. No, he says, those were not the king's reasons; the king wished to escape "the Order's heavy chains" and be free! A hard lesson has, however, been learned, and the king is back with the church; but, says the Inquisitor,

> "If I did not
> Stand now before you—by the living God!
> You would have stood before me thus tomorrow."

Why, he asks, has the king summoned him, anyway? Hesitantly the king comes to that point: his only son has planned rebellion and he is uncertain whether to let him flee the country or to put him to death. Can the Inquisitor condone the latter course?

"To expiate eternal Righteousness
God's own son died upon the cross."

Can the Inquisitor convey that idea throughout Europe?

"As far as they adore the cross."

But does the action not go contrary to Nature?

"Before the Faith
No voice of Nature has validity."

The king says this is his only son, and asks: "What have I labored for?" The Inquisitor replies:

"For moldering death, before
Such freedom."

"Come, then," says the king, "to receive your victim."
The brief final scene (V, 3) brings Carlos in mask and monk's garb to the queen's door at midnight. Softly they speak of Posa's memory, and Carlos, addressing her as "Mother," renounces passionate love for filial devotion. He is about to leave Spain until such time as he can return as its king. He will not write to her until he has reached Ghent. The clock strikes twelve. He reaches for the mask he has briefly put down, saying, "Let this have been my last deceit." "It is your last one," says the king, stepping forth from the shadows. The queen faints, and Carlos seizes her up into his arms. To the Grand Inquisitor behind him the king says: "Cardinal! I have done what my part required. Do your part now."
The curtain falls.
This shattering close is a plummet plunge to total

darkness beyond all hope. The ultimate fates of Carlos and the queen are all the more gruesome for being left mysterious. This Act V will stand comparison for tragic grandeur with Shakespeare, with Euripides, and with Racine. By itself, apart from the rest of the play, it is the greatest thing Schiller ever wrote.

Interpretations

In the Romantic era *Don Carlos* was construed as "a Don Carlos play" and famous actors coveted the title role. Attention centered on a splendid young prince crushed by the tyranny of his father and king, a diagnosis closely parallel to that famous Goethean diagnosis of Hamlet that is set forth in *Wilhelm Meister*. Modern audiences and readers find such a role unpalatable, the hero is too passive, he suffers too much, he does not *do* anything. Hamlet, hedged about on all sides, is still a shrewd and dangerous opponent and, on occasion, given to swift violence of action, but Carlos, as a Man of Feeling, is too meek, too sensitive. The objection cannot be refuted, though under the circumstances it is difficult to see what he could do.

Very easily, however, *Don Carlos* can become "a King Philip play" and has so become in its stage history. This King Philip offers a magnificent role. Somber, melancholy, and jealous, he is also possessed of quick intelligence, perceptiveness, and occasional magnanimity, as when in III, 2 he readily forgives his admiral who has just lost the Armada. He bears well the crushing weight of his own solemn decorum—as Louis XIV bore his. Yet his heart is parched, and a sympathetic actor can make his impulse to affection and humanity very moving. His fall from love down to the bottomless pit of hate is a shattering spectacle. No less shattering, though underlined by irony, is the moment when he, the mightiest monarch on earth, learns that he is the helpless puppet of the Grand Inquisitor.

The women play accessory roles. Eboli is a conventional villainess and intriguer, whose genuine remorse is a trifle implausible though it fits well into the overall quality of the play. The queen has a dignity beyond any previous heroine of Schiller's, as well as a certain intellectual quality by virtue of her support of liberal ideas, but for the most part she is gentle and sweet. She was surely intended to be of a lyric loveliness. Neither woman, however, can possibly dominate the play.

In the second half of the nineteenth century, *Don Carlos* tended to become "a Marquis of Posa play," with emphasis on the message of political idealism. Given that conception, the role is a difficult one to cast. Posa cannot be much older than Carlos—twenty-three—for they were childhood playmates (line 156) and fellow-students at Alcalá, and it is possible to read Alba's account of him in III, 2 to signify that he is no more than nineteen. Yet, he must have feats of bravery behind him and he must be able to cope intellectually with the astute monarch. That his ideals are those of 1787 and inconceivable in 1568 is a point of no importance, but his exuberant idealism may come off as the talk of a bright boy astonishing his grandfather.

As late as 1935 his famous line "Give us freedom of thought!" drew audience applause. A Nazi newspaper editorial rebuked the audience, insisting that Schiller outgrew the oversimplifications of Posa, who knew only the choice between tyranny and democracy. That twisted half-truth, with its sly pseudo-Platonic use of the word "democracy," may be compared with the half-truth of Nietzsche's devastating comment about Schiller's being "a moral Trumpeter of Säckingen"—*The Trumpeter of Säckingen* being a popular and facile nineteenth-century verse narrative. Almost certainly Nietzsche had Posa in mind, and the remark is grossly unfair to both Posa and Schiller. It came, we believe, from the error of taking *Don Carlos* as "a Marquis of Posa play" with a pretentious message of edification.

Twentieth-century interpretations have abandoned the notions of "a Don Carlos play," "a King Philip play," and "a Marquis of Posa play." Occasionally the work has been forced into the mold of a revolutionary play, but most directors have construed it as a family tragedy, basing that idea on Schiller's own note that termed it "a family portrait in a princely house." That footnote of the dramatist's, however, was made à propos of the still unfinished prose version—what we have called "the lesser half" of the play and the portion still in the storm-and-stress idiom. There, we believe, the footnote is perfectly apt, but we cannot agree to extending that definition to the completed work of 1787.

Up to line 2940, we understand the play as the story of a middle-aged man who married his son's fiancée and then lived in a misery of jealous suspicion of both those young people. Action is precipitated by Eboli; Alba and Domingo are her accessories. Posa, in his Horatio aspect, is simply the prince's confidant.

But following line 2940, Posa is advanced by the dramatist from secondary to primary importance, and, compensatorily, the queen recedes from primary to secondary importance. The complexities of Act IV result from the dramatist's attempt to have it both ways, but Act V reveals the action as basically a disastrous rivalry of father and son for the friendship of Posa.

Such a theme depends, in part, upon an eighteenth-century literary tradition of heroic and dedicated

friendship, as represented by the Orestes-Pylades dialogue in Goethe's *Iphigenia in Tauris*, Act II, lines
638ff., yet in the present case there is a degree of
emotion that startles us. Carlos's denunciation of the
king in the presence of Posa's corpse goes beyond
moral indignation at a brutal murder, even the brutal
murder of a friend; rather, it is the frenzied taunting
of a rival in love. Nor can the king's apoplectic seizure
then, or his satanic plunge afterwards into cosmic
hatred, be the results of no more than paternal outrage
at a son's defiance or royal outrage at political betrayal; rather, these acts of behavior betoken a subcon-
scious erotic jealousy and a ghastly rage over betrayal
in love. Nowhere does the text suggest any fleshly
expression of passion on the part of any of the three
male personages in question, and Benno von Wiese
stresses the spiritual quality of the Carlos-Posa friendship. Yet in 1788, a year after completion of *Don
Carlos*, Schiller began planning a drama, "The Knights
of Malta" (*Die Malteser*), in which three figures pre-
dominated: a father, a son, and the son's friend, with
an exalted male passion explicit between the son and
his friend—and Posa, in III, 2 (German text, III, 7), is
described as a Knight of Malta and sole survivor from
the siege of that island that is the subject of the pro-
jected new drama.

A *Don Carlos* that took these psychological factors
into consideration would result in a decidedly modern
drama of shattering tragic impact. No stage production
has adopted such an interpretation.

In the twentieth century most directors have followed the late-nineteenth-century tradition of taking
the entire play—not just the first half—as a "family
tragedy" and then spicing it with the interesting conception of King Philip as the querulous December
partner in a May-December marriage. This king has a

dog-in-the-manger attitude relative to his young wife: sexually incompetent himself, he is morbidly jealous of his competent son, and from his frustration stem his petty meanness and his petty cruelty to one and all. The Berlin Schillertheater's 1955 production dressed this withered and spiteful oldster in black, allowing him a purple cloak at certain moments, and dressed almost all other members of the cast in black, even to a silent chorus of ladies-in-waiting for the queen, all clacking large black fans on cue. These funereal figures then moved about the half-sets and quarter-sets of a revolving stage like ants in a littered cupboard.

While directors continue thus to betray a great drama, the public has happily had access to Verdi's stupendous opera *Don Carlo*, which holds the grandeur of the work intact. Composed in 1867 to a French text, it was extensively revised and reset to an Italian text by Boïto in 1883, when Verdi was at the zenith of his powers. Necessarily it abridged the long play, but the scenes are ingeniously reordered in an acceptable pattern and nothing essential is lacking. Appropriately for the compositional dates, it is essentially "a Philip-and-Posa play," with emphasis on political and religious toleration. Verdi's setting of Posa's line "The peace of cemeteries!" is breathtaking. But significant music is assigned to all five principals: Carlos, the king, the queen, Posa, and Eboli. And no basso is going to sing King Philip as a feeble and petulant old man.

Schiller's play, meanwhile, deserves and awaits a new production that will reveal it as the timeless creation that it is.

Robert Dudley, Earl of Leicester, masks his genuine love
for Mary Stuart by pretending love for Elizabeth Tudor.
When he is all but caught in his treason, he makes a desperate bid for his own safety by suggesting Mary's execution. The skeptical Elizabeth replies by assigning him to be
overseer of the execution. Philip Bosco and Nancy Mar-
chand are here shown in the Leicester and Elizabeth roles
from the Lincoln Center Repertory Theater's 1971–72
production of Schiller's *Mary Stuart*.

Eva Le Gallienne portrayed Queen Elizabeth in the National Repertory Theater's production of *Mary Stuart*, which toured various cities in the 1961–62 season. Shrewd, forceful, conniving, incapable of giving love or of receiving love, the queen here debates with herself whether she dare order the execution of her cousin, rival, and captive, Mary Stuart.

VAN WILLIAMS

In the same National Repertory Theater's 1961–62 production of *Mary Stuart*, Faye Emerson played the role of the young Scottish queen, prisoner of her only living relative, who possesses the throne that Mary Stuart—and half of Europe—claimed in her own right.

VAN WILLIAMS

Highwayman Roller, played by Rudolf Therkatz, tells his companions about his hair's-breadth escape from the gallows in Schiller's *The Robbers*, Act II. The photograph is from the 1951 production of the play in Düsseldorf, under the direction of Gustaf Gründgens.

In the 1951 production of *The Robbers*, Gustaf Gründgens played the role of the villainous Franz Moor as well as directing the production. In Act III he tries to compel the love of Amalia, his absent brother's fiancée, here played by Antje Weisgerber.

In a 1959 production of Schiller's *William Tell* in Düsseldorf, Attilla Hörbiger played the title role and Stephan
Runge played his young son, Walter. Here the father explains to the boy something of the freedom of Swiss life
and something of the non-freedom of life in lands far
downstream from them. A few minutes later Tell is arrested for disregarding the law of the capricious tyrant-
governor.

The tyrant Gessler, played by Ernst Deutsch in the 1959 production of *William Tell* in Düsseldorf, orders the famous marksman to shoot an apple off his young son's head at eighty paces. "Here is my heart!" implores Tell. "Call to your mounted men and mow me down!" To which Gessler replies, "I do not want your life, I want this shot."

The interview between King Philip II of Spain and the Grand Inquisitor belongs among the very greatest scenes in drama. In the play *Don Carlos*, it comes as the second-last scene, but in Verdi's operatic version, which offers music to match Schiller's grandeur, the interview is shifted to a somewhat earlier point in the work. The picture shown here is from the Metropolitan Opera's 1950–51 revival of Verdi's *Don Carlo* as staged by Margaret Webster, with Cesare Siepi in the role of King Philip and Jerome Hines as the Grand Inquisitor.

Wallenstein

After neglecting dramatic composition for ten years Schiller set to work on his longest and greatest work, his trilogy of dramas collectively entitled *Wallenstein*, completing the project in just over two years' time, a feat that would not have been possible without the four agonizing years spent on *Don Carlos* and on "finding himself" as an artist.

Settled since 1787 in Jena and contentedly married since early in 1790, Schiller was engaged in 1791 in writing his *History of the Thirty Years' War*, and, as he wrote, the thought occurred to him that a tragic drama might well be built around the figure of Albrecht Wallenstein, the General of the Imperial and Catholic army who was assassinated in 1634, midway through the conflict. Letters of 1791 and 1792 mention such a project, but if any tentative prose sketches were made in 1793, they have been lost. It was Goethe's enthusiastic encouragement that led Schiller to announce "work begun" on March 21, 1796, but serious composition did not really begin until 1797. The total work emerged as follows:

> *Prologue*—a prefatory poem of 138 lines, composed October 2, 1798, with refer-

ence primarily to the circumstances of the premiere but regularly printed as part of the trilogy text.

Wallenstein's Camp (Wallensteins Lager)—(first entitled "Prologue," then "Wallenstein's Men"), composed January–June 1797 but with additions up to September 30, 1798. Premiere October 12, 1798.

The Piccolomini (Die Piccolomini)—completed November 11, 1798, but with revisions up to December 31. This version comprised *The Piccolomini* plus Acts I and II of *The Death of Wallenstein*. Premiere January 30, 1799.

The Death of Wallenstein (Wallensteins Tod)—consisting originally of only Acts III, IV, and V of the final text; completed March 17, 1799. Premiere April 20, 1799.

The entire trilogy was published as a two-volume work in June of 1800 and rapidly sold out an edition of four thousand copies.

In contrast to the experience with *Don Carlos*, elaborate historical research preceded dramatic composition or even the intention for dramatic composition, so that there was no disconcerting discovery in mid-course of false assumptions about the hero. The seventeenth-century events might have been known to audiences of 1797–99 in about the degree that modern Americans might know about the Civil War and Generals Grant and Lee, but the subject was chosen for no reasons of nostalgic patriotism but solely because the facts of Wallenstein's case seemed to Schiller to be inherently dramatic. Moreover, the trilogy was to be his only drama on a subject drawn from German history. Nor was there any intention of composing a period piece to exploit the picturesqueness of a bygone era. Schiller's aim was to lift the subject matter into timelessness and to invest it with mythic qualities.

At the outset we may define this work as being ultimately a dramatic myth about the universal theme of loyalty and treachery.

The Thirty Years' War

In 1618 the smoldering fire of religious conflict burst into raging flame that no one could control, and it was to rage for thirty years. The war began in Prague when the Protestant faction installed a Protestant king on the vacant Bohemian throne against the will of the Holy Roman Emperor in Vienna. The new monarch, as predicted, ruled only through the winter of 1618–19 and then fled, bearing with him the nickname of "the Winter King." A major Catholic victory of November 8, 1620, had the appearance of ending the struggle, but sullen guerilla fighting by the Protestants went on for another five years. In 1625 King Christian IV of Denmark decided to come to the aid of his fellow religionists, and the Viennese court wondered in dismay how it could finance opposition to him.

At that juncture a private individual made the emperor an astoundingly generous offer. Albrecht Waldstein, or Wallenstein, overlord of the district of Friedland in Bohemia and a Catholic convert from Lutheranism, proposed to recruit 20,000 men, pay them out of his personal fortune, and put them at the emperor's disposal. There was nothing to do but accept, though acceptance embarrassed the emperor, galled his generals, and led bigots to question the good faith of the convert.

The wealth of Wallenstein attracted more nearly 30,000 men than 20,000, and at the head of these troops he drove Protestant General Mansfeld all the way from eastern Germany to Hungary and there defeated him utterly in 1627. For each success the emperor rewarded him with new titles, new authority, and new grants of lands. Next, heading north, where General Tilly had merely held the Danes at bay, Wallenstein invaded Denmark, conquered the whole country, and permitted the Danish king to continue rule only on the condition that he meddle no further in the war. For the second time, it looked as though the Catholic powers had a decisive victory.

But then the Swedes intervened where the Danes had failed. In 1630 King Gustavus Adolphus, personally commanding 12,000 Swedes, landed on the Baltic coast of the Germanies. Precisely then the emperor yielded to the jealous pressures of his advisors and relieved Wallenstein of his command. Wallenstein quietly withdrew to his estates and the Swedish armies advanced straight toward the heart of German territory. Other Protestant states took to arms; Brandenburg, Saxony, Weimar, and Catholic France supported them with money! Cardinal Richelieu, head of the French state under Louis XIII, could not tolerate encirclement of his country by the Holy Roman Empire, Catholics though both might be, and he chose to help the Protestant cause for political reasons.

In October, 1631, the emperor's representatives were begging Wallenstein to resume command. Wallenstein refused. So again in November. In December he agreed to raise a new army but refused to lead it. By April, 1632, the magic of his name had recruited between 40,000 and 50,000 men, but still he refused to command them. Just then General Tilly was killed in battle. Appeals to Wallenstein now became frantic. This time he gave in, but on such terms that little more than his personal word was left to make him responsible to the emperor.

Almost immediately he recaptured Bohemia. Then

he marched against the Swedes, and after a bewildering pause of nine weeks during which he did nothing at all, he inflicted a defeat, but not a decisive defeat, on them and then marched away. His maneuvers in the course of the rest of 1632 and 1633 baffled everyone, and though he had successes, he chose repeatedly to conclude terms with the enemy without consulting Vienna.

Anxiety at the Vienna court was at fever pitch. Wallenstein's army was the only army at the emperor's disposition. There was no money to raise another. Wallenstein's men were loyal only to him, because he and he alone paid them. It was openly said that he was planning to abandon the Catholic cause and make a peace over the heads of all parties belligerent. There was speculation that he planned to make himself emperor—and perhaps assassinate the entire imperial family. In Vienna it became the fixed resolution to stop him at all costs, by murder if necessary.

Schiller's drama opens at this point, and it condenses events of the winter months of 1633–34 into four days' time, ending with the assassination of Wallenstein on the night of February 25, 1634. (The war raged on until 1648.)

Wallenstein's Camp

Novelty, curiosity, and local pride attracted the capacity audience to the new Weimar Theater on October 12, 1798, but it must be admitted that only the special circumstances of the occasion made the program viable. First, the spectators saw Kotzebue's justifiably forgotten piece, *The Corsicans*; then they heard Schiller's 138-line Prologue, which formally presented the new building to them; and finally they saw the play they had come to see, *Wallenstein's Camp*. The Prologue informed them that the titular hero would not appear until a subsequent drama.

No matter what short piece is double-billed with *Wallenstein's Camp*, the program will be unsatisfactory. The work rouses interest but fails to satisfy that interest. It is a good beginning, but only a beginning. The difficulty lies with the idea of trilogies. Schiller had in mind the *Oresteia* of Aeschylus, but that admirable model is divided into three nearly equal parts designed for consecutive performance on a single day. Shakespeare's four history plays, *Richard II*, Parts I and II of *Henry IV*, and *Henry V*, are four independent works only loosely associated in a sequence. In two Schiller-influenced trilogies, Grillparzer's *The Golden Fleece* (1821) and Hebbel's *The Nibelungs* (1861), the dramatists combined a one-act Part I with a four-act Part II to occupy a first evening and assigned a five-act Part III to a second evening. Schiller followed none of these procedures, so that rescue of his fine Part I depends on crowding it together with *The Piccolominis* in a single performance.

At the premiere our long one-acter began with a soldiers' chorus, no longer included in the text, which was heard before, during, and for a couple of minutes after the raising of the curtain. The audience then saw a morning scene in the camp of Wallenstein, Duke of Friedland. A peasant, accompanied by his son, is sizing up possible gamesters on whom to use a pair of loaded dice. A cavalry sergeant and a trumpeter discuss the significant news that Wallenstein's duchess and daughter are to arrive in camp today and the fact that the various units under the general's command are also being assembled here in one camp. They also mention, with dislike, the imperial inspector (Questenberg) who has been "stalking the camp since yesterday." A sharpshooter is tricking a Croat in an unfair swap of possessions. A sutlerwoman tells of the hardships of following an army about. A field-school master marches small boys off to the field school. A very green recruit is eagerly joining up and soldiers ridicule a civilian for trying to prevent the enlistment. In short, we see a motley and not entirely edifying crew of a seventeenth-century army.

For the stage décor, Goethe and Schiller examined old prints and sought to invest the scene with some antiquarian picturesqueness. All dialogue is cast in *Knittelvers*, that rugged tetrameter doggerel, rhymed in pairs, triplets, or quatrains, which Goethe had used to such good effect in *Faust*.

As groups of soldiers gather in conversation we pick up piecemeal a good deal of information about the political and military situation and about the commander-in-chief, and we also see how these men are devoted to Wallenstein and care very little about the emperor's authority. As line 118 of the Prologue stated: "His camp alone will make his [Wallenstein's] crime quite clear." But some of the speeches philosophize about military life, about war and peace, and other topics, because Schiller wished the unnamed soldier types to serve the function of the chorus in Greek drama. The First Cuirassier generalizes at some length on the nature of life in "this man's army." If there are regrettable aspects, he says,

> "I'm truly sorry, so say I.
> But I cannot change it. —You see, it's just
> Like when we make an attack or thrust:
> The horses are snorting and race to the charge,
> Whoever then lies in my path at large,
> My brother, my very son though he be,
> Though his piteous cry rend the soul of me,

> Over his body I must ride,
> I cannot carry him gently aside."

A rare bit of Schillerian humor brings a Capuchin friar among the soldiers (lines 483–622) to preach an angry sermon against their improper way of life. The men listen to his quotations and free translations from Latin scripture and tolerate his outrageous puns, all in the authentic manner of the seventeenth-century preacher Abraham a Santa Clara. "Another Commandment," says the Capuchin, "is: Thou shalt not steal."

> "Well, that one you follow quite literally,
> You carry things off when all can see.
> From your vulture claws and talon vises,
> From your rascals' tricks and your rascals' devices,
> Cash is not safe in the till where it hides,
> The calf is not safe in the cow's insides,
> You take the egg and the hen besides."

Eventually he swells his theme to inveigh against Wallenstein himself:

> "He's a downright Nebuchadnezzar for pride,
> An arch-sinner, a heretic deep-dyed,
> And he goes by the name of Wallenstein . . ."

and then the men grow angry, too, and drive him away.

In the last part of the soldiers' discussion we become aware of the Europe-wide assortment of nationalities in this mercenary army and of the fact that loyalty to Wallenstein is the sole bond that holds them all together. Mention is also made of the popularity of one particular commander, the junior Piccolomini, Max. The talkative First Cuirassier sums the matter up:

"Let every regiment then inscribe
A *Pro Memoria* bold and plain:
All together we mean to remain,
And any force or trick they think of
To drive us from Friedland will be in vain,
For he bears his soldiers a father's love.
This we shall tender in humble devotion
To Piccolomini—I mean the son—
He knows how to handle these things with skill
And with Friedland he can do as he will;
He also has an ace in the hole
With the King and the Emperor at the other pole."

All agree that such a *Pro Memoria* be sent to Wallenstein and that the younger Piccolomini shall take
their message of unqualified support. Then, with good
will overflowing, a martial song is struck up in which
everyone joins. The singing continues even after the
curtain has slowly descended.

Part I of the trilogy, as the broad base of Schiller's
dramatic pyramid, has presented the men; Part II, *The
Piccolominis*, will deal with the officers; Part III, *The
Death of Wallenstein*, will concentrate on the commander-in-chief. Both of the latter are five-act dramas
in blank verse, and in Schiller's second and final ar-
rangement, *The Piccolominis* is limited to one day's
time, the same day as the action of *Wallenstein's Camp*
and the first of the four days of the total drama.

The Piccolominis: *Act I*

"You're late—but still you're here," the text begins,
as General Illo welcomes two fellow commanders, Isolani and Buttler, to headquarters, in the gathering together of all of Wallenstein's regimental leaders. Buttler, however, reports that Count Gallas means not to

come. Immediately we perceive that Wallenstein plans some significant move and that there has already been at least one defection to hamper his plan. Octavio Piccolomini, in company with the imperial negotiator Questenberg, joins the others, and Illo at once waxes hostile. The hostility is eventually seconded by Isolani and then by Buttler, so that when the deputy from Vienna is finally left alone with Octavio Piccolomini he bursts forth in despair: these men will never accept orders from the emperor. Octavio admits that imperial authority gets small respect here, but, double agent that he is, he assures Questenberg that all is not lost, and he cites several factors in Vienna's favor; besides, Wallenstein has not yet come to open rebellion. But then comes the younger Piccolomini, Max, fresh from escorting Wallenstein's womenfolk to camp. From his unwonted excitement and from his quick hostility to Questenberg, his father guesses, rightly, that he is in love with Wallenstein's daughter, Thekla, and with alarm guesses further that his son is being deliberately enticed, by the hope of such a marriage, to remain on Wallenstein's side in the momentous decision that is to be made. "A curse, a threefold curse upon this journey!" cries Octavio as he leads Questenberg off to Wallenstein's audience chamber.

These 606 lines of dialogue are splendid. Key roles are swiftly established, vital information is effortlessly conveyed, and curiosity is whetted by partial disclosure of conflict not fully understood yet but approaching a climax. Yet, in the last analysis, there is only dialogue. Six male characters meet and talk, first three of them, then five, then three, then two—and that is all. We see nothing. A diehard neoclassicist might well ask whether this new dramaturgy was new only in the substitution of seventeenth-century Europeans for Greeks and Romans on stage.

Nor does the elaborate stage set serve any dramatic purpose. Except for one trifling allusion to it in lines 12–13, the six characters might equally well speak in front of a neutral gray curtain. As in *Don Carlos*, action, with a couple of exceptions, tends to move from palace room to palace room, until the overtaxed stage manager must have regretted the single *galérie* that served all five acts of a French tragedy. In the desirable jointure of *The Piccolominis* in a single performance with *Wallenstein's Camp*, we feel that this Act I could easily be set "in another part of the camp," thereby smoothing the transition while relieving the scenic monotony of interiors. It would be possible, we believe, also to prune away parts of Max Piccolomini's long speeches.

The Piccolominis: *Act II*

Act II is more diversified. The initial scene presents, in a mere twenty-six lines, Wallenstein's court astrologer, Seni—a historical personage—in some hocuspocus as he directs the ordering of chairs in the hall. Schiller intended here something mysterious and eerie, with a suggestion of "fateful stars," but he so disliked the "grotesque nonsense" (*die Fratze*) that he spoiled his own spooky effect. Some of the most haplessly unpoetic lines he ever composed are here assigned to the servants accompanying Seni as they ridicule the wizard and his arts.

As Seni leaves the hall, Wallenstein enters in private talk with his duchess, who has just come from Vienna. At court, she relates, her husband's enemies accuse him of treason and her own closest friends hold aloof from her with "solemn ceremoniousness." She is a timid, ineffectual woman, this duchess, and she has the first mother role since the vapid Mrs. Miller. More significantly, she is wholly of Schiller's creation. The play makes no mention of Wallenstein's first wife, the elderly widow from whom his vast fortune derived, so that the present duchess seems to correspond to his second wife, who, though devoted to him, knew nothing of his plans and was not with him in the last weeks of his life.

Upon the husband-wife discussion enters the Countess Terzky, bringing with her Wallenstein's lovely daughter, Thekla, who has not seen her father for many years and who has just been brought from her convent by Max Piccolomini. This Countess Terzky is the sister of the duchess, hence Wallenstein's sister-in-law, and the wife of the conspirator Count Terzky. The relationships have been modified from historical fact, but by conferring aspects of Lady Macbeth upon the Countess Terzky and aspects of Macbeth upon Wallenstein, Schiller has created some odd psychological problems. As for Thekla, the heroine of the play, she is an independent fiction with no basis in history at all, except insofar as Wallenstein did have a daughter, named Marie, who was ten years old in 1634.

Count Terzky now joins the little family gathering, and when the women have withdrawn, General Illo comes in. In the play, as in history, Illo is the ringleader of the conspiracy. Terzky, who in history had only a minor conspiratorial role, is here hand-in-glove with Illo.

At line 1010 other commanders enter the hall and presently there is opened the formal hearing of Questenberg, the envoy from the emperor.

Suddenly our play kindles into dramatic flame. As Wallenstein and Questenberg argue their points of view, the audience is caught up in the fierce duel of will against will and mind against mind. Clearly, resolution is out of the question. This verbal battle cannot but pass over into armed conflict. To the fair-minded listener, this Questenberg is a shifty special pleader, and we feel the emperor who sent him is a scoundrel. Wallenstein has been shamefully used, as he convincingly demonstrates—until line 1260. Then comes one of those breath-taking strokes of Schiller's genius. Just when Wallenstein has won every opinion to his side, he veers off into that other sector of his personality where all is calculation, falseness, and egotism. With detestable insincerity, which is patent to the audience but which persuades the generals, he launches into a maudlin speech about his grief over what will become of his loyal officers and men if the emperor has his way. He clowns his grief like a cynical charlatan, and as they all loudly protest their devotion to him he stands smugly triumphant as the splendid scene closes.

Here is head-on dramatic collision of a very exciting kind. The tableau of listening officers should be staged in terms of eighteenth-century oil paintings of generals and their staffs. Let us note the effect of a play within a play, as the two principals duel it out and the staff officers watch. When, at the end, the tableau dissolves into movement and outcry, there is realized a vivid symbol of the audience's own excitement.

Questenberg, meanwhile, must be seen as a good deal more than an "old geezer . . . from Vienna with his golden chain" (*Wallenstein's Camp*, lines 70–71). He is worsted, it is true, but we need to remember that Wallenstein and his generals have incited *us* to mutiny, whereas Questenberg stands for law and order, forces yet to be reckoned with.

The historical counterpart of this scene was twofold: Count Trautmannsdorf's mission in December, 1633, and Father Quiroga's mission of January 5, 1634. In combining those two foes of Wallenstein into one,

Schiller oddly assigned to the substitute the name of Questenberg, who was a doggedly loyal supporter of the general.

The Piccolominis: *Act III*

In "a room," Illo is outlining to Terzky a device to get Wallenstein to break his noncommittal silence about their conspiracy and declare his intentions. At the generals' banquet shortly to begin, he will circulate a pledge of allegiance to Wallenstein within the limitations of the soldiers' oath to the emperor. This he will do before dinner. But after dinner, when the generals are over their wine, he will circulate for signature a document that looks exactly like the first one but that will not contain the clause about the oath of loyalty. The signers may later protest the deception to their hearts' content, but at court no one will believe them and they will be left with no choice but to support Wallenstein.

When Illo has left, Countess Terzky tells her husband that their own little subconspiracy is thriving: Max and Thekla are in love. Marriage may or may not ensue, but Max is thus bound to support Wallenstein. Terzky shows Max in, and the countess listens with gratification to the young man's professions of rapture.

Their conversation is partly overheard by Thekla as she stands in the doorway, seen by the countess and the audience but unseen by Max. (We recall how King Philip silently observed the Marquis of Posa in *Don Carlos* III, 3.) Thekla, radiantly lovely and without jewels, must be simply garbed in white, suggestive of an angel. (In 1798 this costume was likely to be termed "ideal," meaning "Grecian," and doubtlessly resembled Jacques Louis David's 1800 painting of Mlle. Charlotte du Val d'Ognes.)

So long as the countess is chaperone, the lovers' meeting is conducted in all propriety, but when she leaves them for a moment, Thekla quickly exclaims: "Don't trust them. They are not sincere." Bred in a convent she may have been, but love has made her aware, and if she does not understand the people around her, she senses their falseness and fore-senses disaster to her love.

While the countess hurries Max off to the banquet, Thekla has a little *scena* to herself, during which she takes up a guitar and sings a song. Perhaps a modern production would shorten the interval of time by having her merely pluck listlessly at the strings of the instrument. The countess returns, and the dialogue between the two women brings out sharp self-defense from the girl. The act closes with a monologue by Thekla, which is imitated from operatic practice and may easily be seen to consist of unrhymed recitative, eight rhymed lines of aria, and six lines of coda. A family doom is mentioned, and "a house . . . destined to destruction," the allusion obviously setting the annihilation of "the house of Wallenstein" parallel to "the house of Atreus."

Schiller composed this Act III *last* and by it he set great store. Max and Thekla, both characters of his own invention, were, he remarked, "the two figures for whom alone I have an affection." This Act III was to be an interlude of warmth in what he feared might otherwise prove a cold, political play, a *Staatsaktion*, about heartless and repugnant people. This pair of youthful lovers, pure, devoted, and poised at the verge of doom, reflect the similar pair, Britannicus and Junie, in Act III, Scene 7 of Racine's *Britannicus*. But where Britannicus momentarily doubted, no shadow of doubt crosses the love of Max for Thekla. Indeed, more important than their love for each other is their loyalty to each other in this large drama about loyalties and betrayals.

The Piccolominis: *Act IV*

Amid the brilliance of Act IV, the originality of its stage procedures may escape notice. The décor of Act I we described as irrelevant; that of Act II differed little from the French classical *galérie*, save that chairs were placed and numerous characters were seated; that of Act III were merely "a room." But in Act IV a banquet is specified, with three tables, thirty seated commanders, servants who serve, and musicians who play their music as they circulate before all the tables. One needs to recall that in Greek drama, as in Racine, such a scene was unthinkable. In *Britannicus* there is a banquet, but it had to be reported in a messenger speech by Burrhus (V, 5). There is also a banquet scene in *Macbeth* (III, 4), but it must have been simulated with minimum furnishings on the inner stage and it lasted only 121 lines, after which a curtain must have been closed to allow the principals to continue their conversation out on the main stage, as though they were coming away from the dinner. Even Goethe's *Götz von Berlichingen* (I, 4) required no more than a decked table and a few chairs that could almost instantly be removed. But in *Piccolominis*, Act IV, the elaborate setting serves for an entire act, it is an integral part of the action, and the opulence of its gold plate, crystal, and lighted chandeliers is "atmospheric" in a way that anticipates nineteenth-century stage procedures.

The historical counterpart of Act IV was the officers' banquet of January 12, 1634, here advanced to the fourth evening before February 25. Action centers on the circulation of that document that omitted the clause about the soldiers' oath, as described by Illo previously. It is crucial for his plans that everyone sign it. The previous document with the oath has already been shown around. In history there was only one document; it contained the clause; it still exists, and it is endorsed by two Piccolominis, but not the father-son pair of our play. Schiller, however, knew of the old rumor of two documents, and he put the rumor to excellent dramatic use.

Midway through Act IV a long conversation takes place, well downstage near the resplendent buffet, between the Cellar Master and Neumann, Wallenstein's adjutant. What they say is interesting enough, and their information about the war and other matters is interesting enough, but an audience will probably listen only in snatches, because attention will follow the by-play of the signing of the document by some thirty persons. A director's ingenuity will be taxed to provide variety here, but he must see to it that tension mounts steadily from signer to signer.

It was the objective of the two Terzkys in their subconspiracy to distract Max with the interview with Thekla to the point where he would sign almost anything. In good Schillerian fashion, the loveless Terzkys miscalculate the effects of love, so that Max now refuses to sign anything at all until a calmer time. His father signs, because as double agent he knows he can escape the consequences at court, but he declines to press his son to do so. The drunken Illo is furious and blurts out much of the truth about the false document together with his personal antipathy for both Piccolominis, and his words would undo him and his conspiracy simultaneously, were it not that everyone is to some degree in his cups. When he draws a dagger and seeks to force Max to sign, Max easily wrests the weapon away and the magnificent scene dissolves in general uproar.

The Piccolominis: *Act V*

If Acts IV and V are both relatively short, it is because they were designed as two scenes of a single act, for at the 1798 premiere, the play extended to what is now the end of Act II of *The Death of Wallenstein*. Where the banquet scene was public, social, loud, and full of movement, the present scene shows a private room lighted by a single lamp. The time is late in the night following the dinner. Octavio Piccolomini is confronting his son with the evidence of the treasonable conspiracy:

> "The Duke pretends he is about to leave
> The army; at this juncture they propose
> A plan—to steal the army from the Emperor
> And lead it over to the enemy."

Max denounces this "priest-hatched tale." Octavio names names and expounds at greater length. Max dismisses the facts as coincidences, asserting that Wallenstein knows nothing of such a plot. His father says Wallenstein himself broached the plot to him; his son insists there must be some mistake and he blames his father for betraying confidences. Gradually Octavio reveals that he is a spy for the emperor and produces a secret imperial order authorizing Wallenstein's murder and appointing himself as commander-in-chief, though the order is to be activated only when and if Wallenstein perpetrates treason openly. Max is confident that such a moment will never come, declaring, in a very Schillerian line: "Your judgment can be wrong, but not my heart."

Just then a courier is announced from Count Gallas, one of the few generals who has failed to come to headquarters at Wallenstein's summons. The courier's message is oral: Sesina, Wallenstein's go-between with the enemy, has been captured with documentary proof, in Terzky's handwriting, of the commander-in-chief treasonable dealings.

With proof in hand, Octavio is aghast to hear his son declare that he will go for clarification to Wallenstein himself, thereby destroying all that diplomacy has laboriously accomplished. In the quintessentially Schillerian speech that ends the play, Max replies:

"O this diplomacy, how I abhor it!
By your diplomacy you will yet force him
To take a step—Yes, you would go so far as *make*
Him guilty just because you *want* him guilty.
O this can have none but an evil end.—
Let it resolve itself whichever way
It may, I sense disaster looming near.—
For when he falls, this kingly man will pull
A world to its destruction down with him,
And like a ship which in the middle ocean
All of a sudden catches fire and bursts
Aloft and instantaneously casts all
The crew it bore out into sea and sky
So we, who in his fortunes are involved,
Shall all be carried down in his collapse.
    You may proceed as you see fit; grant *me*
However, leave to act in my own fashion.
Between this man and me all must be pure,
And I must learn before this hard day's end
Whom I must sacrifice, my father or my friend."

Here is the outcry of the moral conscience and the intuitive heart in opposition to all that is calculation, dissimulation, and expediency. Here is the uniquely Schillerian conflict of "idealist" versus "realist." Here is Schiller's art at its noblest and best.

The father-son opposition that emerges in the latter stages of *The Piccolominis* has been a prominent theme in all of Schiller's plays to date, except in *Fiesco*. It will continue into the third part of the trilogy, but thereafter it will disappear from the completed plays. It occurs in the present work with no basis in historical fact save for the signatures of two Piccolominis, who were not father and son, on that document circulated at the historical banquet of January 12, 1634. There was an actual Octavio Piccolomini, but in 1634 he was thirty-three years of age and unmarried. Most of his political role was played by Count Gallas, who here is an offstage character. He was highly regarded by Wallenstein, especially for his bravery at the battle of Lützen on November 16, 1632, but the special and superstitious trust in him on the part of the stage Wallenstein is Schiller's invention, and it regards once again the overall dramatic theme of loyalty and treachery. Max, on the other hand, is wholly fictional, though the historical Wallenstein had a favorite nephew, Max von Waldstein, who inherited his personal fortune. We may also mention that the historical Sesina, who served as Terzky's messenger to the Swedes, was never captured by anybody and that he later purchased his own safety by detailed confession of all his transactions.

The Death of Wallenstein

Without *The Piccolominis*, the opening of *The Death of Wallenstein* is abrupt and the play forfeits the breadth of character portrayal that has been so carefully prepared, yet, trilogies being what they are,

this part III has often been performed as an independent drama. German-language audiences may bring to
the work enough background information from their
school days to make everything comprehensible, but
other people might be confused. On the other hand,
this Part III has advantages: the focus is now clearly
on Wallenstein himself, the moment of forced decision sets the action off at a rapid sweep, dramatic tension is higher, and a definitive conclusion is reached.

The curtain rises on the interesting décor of the
astrological tower, which Thekla described at some
length in *Piccolominis* III, but Schiller was again embarrassed apparently by "the grotesque nonsense" and
has Wallenstein draw a curtain before the "images" of
the planets after a mere thirty-nine lines of dialogue
with Seni. Thus Terzky, entering excitedly with the
news of Sesina's capture, speaks before a neutral background. Hard on his heels comes Illo to report that the
Swedish colonel has arrived to discuss terms. With
brutal suddenness the moment of decision has come,
and Wallenstein is sufficiently distressed to require a
few minutes to himself. He then speaks an important
eighty-four-line soliloquy.

Wallenstein's Soliloquy and Character

About the general's true intentions the audience has
heard nothing so far, though allegations have been
made, particularly by Octavio Piccolomini. Even
Terzky and Illo are not sure what he means to do.
Speaking now in the privacy of his heart, Wallenstein
admits that he has contemplated taking his entire army
over to the enemy; he further entertains "a royal
hope," which later proves to be the hope of making
himself king of Bohemia, a post that would necessarily
be under the emperor's jurisdiction. Not a word does

he say about the actual rumor of 1634 that claimed that he wanted to make himself emperor and perhaps even assassinate the entire imperial family; not a word about that more plausible rumor of 1634 to the effect that he intended to force a conclusion of the war and establish the principle of religious toleration, which, in Vienna, was anathema. We are disappointed. Schiller, we feel, missed a tremendous opportunity, perhaps from having become overcircumspect in political and religious matters. Would he, we wonder, have missed such a chance back in the days of *Don Carlos*? On this point we are left guessing. In our drama, at any rate, Wallenstein aspires no higher than to a vassal kingship. That post, we fancy, he could have achieved well short of treason, perhaps by merely demanding it, so that we feel the author backed down from a theme too dangerous to handle in 1797–99.

But Wallenstein has contemplated taking his entire army over to the enemy. Now we are startled to hear him say he "never meant it in earnest." He has luxuriated in daydreaming about what he could do if he chose. He is aware of what Illo and Terzky intend; he has countenanced their preparations; he knows what letters Sesina carried; and he knows that without his concurrence nothing can be done. What dismays him at this moment is the fact that he must decide, and immediately, whether to activate the conspiracy or to cancel it once and for all. He decides for the former option, but even as he does so, it has ceased to be an option and has become a necessity. Soon he will be like a lion in a net, dangerous only at the kill.

This behavior, we submit, has its psychological parallel in the figure of the miser that haunts nineteenth-century fiction—Balzac, Dostoevsky, George Eliot, to cite only the most famous authors who interested themselves in this theme. The miser gloats in secret over his gold, glorying in its potential power but is unable to bring himself to part with a single coin; just so, Wallenstein has toyed with his potential power without seriously intending to do anything. We find this character of 1797–99 proto-Romantic in nature.

The reasons for taking his entire army over to the enemy are so obscurely put in the soliloquy that we are tempted to think Wallenstein is a double-dealer even with himself. To the Swedish colonel he will presently claim (line 267) that the emperor forced him to it, and to Max Piccolomini he will say (line 705) that the court was determined to destroy him. In lines 835ff. he will see himself parallel to Julius Caesar, who led his armies against Rome itself. His aspiration to the throne of Bohemia will recur in lines 240, 350–51, 297–99. The reasons resolve themselves, therefore, into: pique, fear of a second removal from office and possibly of assassination, and a limited ambition for the Bohemian kingship.

In part, also, Wallenstein is "typed" as "the ambitious man" by virtue of his literary relationship to Macbeth. That relationship will become clearer in our subsequent analysis.

At the same time we observe an attempt to bring him in line with Aristotle's concept of the tragic hero. That attempt could not be successful, because this protagonist has more evil components in his character than Aristotle could have approved. The tragic flaw in Wallenstein is too broad a band to be termed a mere flaw. Above all, he is of too modern a mentality to fit Aristotle's definition; all these complexities—the double-dealing, the deep-seated dishonesty, the miser-like gloating over potential power—reflect, in our opinion, the proto-Romantic era in which Schiller lived.

Least of all do these psychological complexities have

to do with the historical Albrecht Wallenstein, who was a cold man, aloof from his soldiers and even from his officers, objectively concerned with generalship and diplomacy and with vast projects of administration. In managing his vast estates he displayed severity combined with utter fairness and shrewd common sense. Of personal affections he showed little trace. Around his person he cultivated ostentatious ceremony. He was fond of public pronouncements of his own achievements and of scathing judgments on his rivals and opponents. While his conversion to Catholicism was sincere, he firmly believed in religious toleration. In war he was consistently astute and cautious, rather than picturesquely bold. For all that he was given to astrology, he was a pragmatic economist and an able administrator of mines, factories, trades, and schools. As a husband, he was loyal to his duchess, but he did not confide in her or keep her with him. He was, in short, a man from the Age of Reason, whence Schiller brought him forward into the Age of Sensibility, surrounding him with wife, maiden daughter, affiliates by marriage, foster son, and devoted friend.

The Action as Far as the End of Act II, Scene 2

Once face to face with the Swedish colonel, Wallenstein strikes his treasonable bargain, but no sooner is the colonel gone than he tells Terzky he means to withdraw from the bargain. Then it is that Countess Terzky forces herself upon him and with arguments clearly parallel to those of Lady Macbeth (in I, 7 of Shakespeare's play) brings him around again to carrying out the bargain.

Act II opens with the painful interview between Wallenstein and Max Piccolomini. The latter's impassioned plea for upright procedures makes more of an impression than the general is willing to admit. As soon as Max has left him, he wishes to recall the Swedish colonel, but that emissary has vanished as swiftly as the Evil One. Next we see Wallenstein fondly and wrongheadedly loyal in his defense of Octavio Piccolomini, whom he has dispatched in total trust to bring up the missing regiments and to arrest the leaders who disobeyed him and refused to come to the headquarters at Pilsen.

Act II, Scene 2 is a splendid scene in three sections showing Octavio Piccolomini as a skillful agent in the emperor's interests. First, with Count Isolani, he is able to swing that shallow and venal man in record time from support of Wallenstein to support of the imperial cause. Second, he deftly and cruelly effects the same result with Colonel Buttler. But when he comes to deal with Max, his own son, he meets resistance. Not that Max will support Wallenstein—he has other plans, which we shall discuss presently—but father and son poignantly realize that their paths must henceforth diverge and that they are likely never to see each other again. Only one reproach may be leveled against this scene: it too closely resembles the Octavio-Max interview in *Piccolominis*, V, somewhat as the tumultuous close of *Piccolominis*, IV, too closely resembled the tumultuous close of *Piccolominis*, II. It was a fault of Schiller's to echo his own best scenes. The present father-son interview should, however, be contemplated in the light of what it was originally intended to be, namely the concluding scene of *The Piccolominis*.

Buttler

The compellingly powerful section of II, 2, however, is Octavio's dialogue with Colonel Buttler. Nowhere more than here does *The Death of Wallenstein* suffer in isolation from *The Piccolominis*, for Buttler's role in the ten-act play began, like his life, in obscurity, and from small episode to small episode it has grown into a matter of crucial importance. From illegitimate birth and childhood poverty in Ireland this man has achieved status and fulfillment through Wallenstein, hence he is devoted to the general. Without heirs, he has made the general the beneficiary of his will. There is nothing he would not do for the general, in whose service he has grown gray. But he craves a noble title, has made application for such, and has been refused in Vienna. Deliberately Octavio now shows him Wallenstein's letter to the court recommending that the title not be granted.

We are outraged. Wallenstein cannot have done such a thing. This is a trick of Octavio's. The letter must be a forgery. Wallenstein may be ruthlessly ambitious, he may be treasonable, but with cause. This is wanton treachery against a proved friend. We feel an urge to rush up on stage and demand to inspect that letter for ourselves. (This is not the least tantalizing of Schiller's onstage documents.)

But, alas, the letter is genuine. Octavio is in the right—as usual. Buttler is dumbfounded, crushed. Before our eyes we see the old man's devotion turn to hate. Henceforth he will live for only one purpose: to kill Wallenstein.

The real-life Walter Buttler had origins like those in the play, but he had no such devotion to his general. He engineered Wallenstein's assassination from greed of reward and, to some degree, from his fanatical Catholicism. For his assassin's job he was rewarded with the title of count. The reasons for Schiller's alterations of the role are obvious amid this vast myth of loyalty and betrayal. The Buttler role is a immensely rewarding one, a godsend to an older actor, but we wonder whether it can be truly effective in anything less than the intended ten acts. Its gradual emergence is a literary device more commonly associated with the long prose novel than with a play, and it is a good example of the generalization that Schiller's plays, at least by comparison with French classical drama, have certain aspects of the novel about them.

The Death of Wallenstein: *Act III*

The two long scenes of Act III are full of reverses and disasters. Countess Terzky presses anew her sub-conspiracy by urging Thekla to keep Max and his regiment for her father at all costs, but Wallenstein himself undoes the little plot by declaring he will choose his son-in-law only from among the thrones of Europe. Regimental defections are announced in series, culminating in Octavio's betrayal. Buttler is still on hand, feigning loyalty but actually spying on the general's actions. The duchess is in an anguish of distress. Even Countess Terzky grants that all is lost. From a room in the duchess's quarters, where these events have taken place, we pass to a larger room in the general's quarters for III, 2, probably by the mere lifting of the midstage curtain.

A platoon of soldiers deputized from Max's regiment come to the general to obtain his plain statement: is he, or is he not, about to take the army over to the enemy? Wallenstein begs their question with skillful talk, until Buttler hurries in to announce that Terzky's men have ripped the imperial emblems off their standards and are affixing Wallenstein's own emblems; whereupon the platoon files out without a word. Then follows a grand operalike finale when Max comes to take his farewells. Rebuffed by all for deserting his general, he at last asks for Thekla's opinion. She bids him follow the dictates of his heart, which cannot be false. Gradually the stage fills with his men, who will not allow him to be detained by force and who are prepared to follow wherever he may lead. Offstage horns summon him and them to their destiny. Anglo-Saxons are likely to object to the stylized *tutti*, which does everything that an opera does except break into concerted song—as in the sextette from *Lucia di Lammermoor*—but the scene is no less grand for that.

Max Piccolomini

Max Piccolomini's dilemma may be stated as a syllogism, and Schiller almost certainly conceived of it in just such a tripartite formula: a) he will not betray his oath of loyalty to the emperor by serving Wallenstein; b) he will not betray his heart's loyalty to Wallenstein, his second father; therefore, c) he must die. He is still free to choose the manner of his death, however, and he chooses to lead his regiment against the first enemy contingent he meets before the decision between conflicting loyalties is forced upon him. He must do so at once.

As a martyr to the moral conscience, Max represents the type known to German literature of the 1780s and 1790s as the "beautiful soul" (*schöne Seele*), a complex concept found nowhere else and intimately related to a second complex concept, likewise uniquely German and uniquely of that era, the concept of *Menschheit* or *humanitas*. The term *schöne Seele* originated with Goethe, in Book VI of *Wilhelm Meister*, but its clearest and best-known exemplar is the heroine of Goethe's *Iphigenia in Tauris*. The Princess in Goethe's play, *Torquato Tasso*, is a further example. In all three of those literary cases, the *schöne Seele* was a woman, and two real-life women stood as the models for them. The only male, prior to Schiller, was Sarastro, in Mozart's *Magic Flute* (and his smaller-scale counterpart, Pasha Selim, in Mozart's *Abduction from the Seraglio*), but Sarastro was significantly different—and of the preceding generation—in that his *humanitas* was based on reason, not on the promptings of the intuitive heart. Sarastro, moreover, was a man of kingly power who never needed to fear martyrdom. But in Max Piccolomini, Schiller ventured to create a male *schöne Seele*, as supersensitive to the moral imperative as any of Goethe's women, yet unhedged by power as were Sarastro and Pasha Selim, and his intense moral awareness comes from his intuitive heart. Amid reality, Schiller believed, such a male character inevitably becomes a martyr. Yet this character, created solely out of Schiller's imagination, must not suffer passively like a saint, but actively, as a loyal soldier.

As we learn in IV, 2, Max encountered a Swedish contingent and ordered a suicide attack upon it. In trying to jump a defended ditch, his horse was impaled upon an infantryman's pike and threw its rider, so that Max was trampled to death under the hooves of his own cavalry. Even this last grisly detail relates to the overall theme of loyalty and treachery.

The modern reader may ask how Max, if he is so morally sensitive, can be a soldier at all; or how can

Max, to solve his own moral dilemma, lead his entire regiment to share his death. These are simply twentieth-century questions which must not be asked here. Rather, let us note the Baroque grandeur of the reported death scene and also, with no inconsistency, its Euripidean quality, reminiscent of the death of Hippolytus.

Thekla

Once the nature and the death of Max Piccolomini are correctly understood, it becomes easy to define Thekla as the feminine counterpart of Max. Like him, she is wholly the product of Schiller's imagination; like him, she is a *schöne Seele*; like him, she refuses to choose between loyalty to her father and loyalty to her beloved, and therefore she must die. In keeping with Schiller's notions of womanhood, her two choices, father or beloved, lie wholly within "a woman's sphere," but her refusal of both is a moral decision, and it is the moral decision that removes her death from the category of a *Liebestod*. She will die in the near future, that much is clear, and of grief, but the event lies beyond the time limits of the play. We are still a full generation before the love-death of Hero in Grillparzer's *Hero and Leander*, of 1831, and two generations before Wagner's Isolde, of 1865.

Thekla's memorable interview with the Swedish Captain in IV, 2 combines the characteristics of the messenger speech in Euripides's *Hippolytus* with such modern elements as made it viable in the theater of 1799. The Captain's account of Max's death is a heroic poem in miniature, a bravura piece effective on any stage. Fräulein Neubrunn is present during the interview, partly in the character of a French classical *confidante*, partly for the sake of a decorum that now seems quaint, even absurd, yet, after the Captain has left, Thekla has to speak with someone. The stage direction after line 3072 merits comment. There Thekla covers her face by lowering her veil. Behind that stage direction lie the principles of Lessing's *Laocoon*, which claimed that a statue (or painting) must not represent the subject in extreme pain or joy, because the contorted features in fixed position become grotesque. In this deliberately "Greek" scene, Thekla is like a living statue. (We glimpse the Goethe-Schiller method of direction.) Effective too is the imitation of Greek stichomythia in the exchange between Thekla and Fräulein Neubrunn and between Thekla and the equerry. Here, not full lines, but half-lines and double lines alternate between speakers, giving the (non-Greek) effect of intense and barely suppressed emotion.

Thekla's monologue (lines 3155–80), like the one at the end of *Piccolominis*, III, is an aria, elegiac in tone this time, consisting of six unrhymed lines of recitative, two rhymed octets (with one line too short), and a quatrain of coda. In this coda we distinguish Schiller's own voice:

> "And then comes Fate. —Brutal and cold
> It snatches my Belovèd's gracious mold
> And under the hooves of horses has him hurled.—
> Such is the lot of Beauty in the world."

The tiny role of the equerry is a master stroke. By offering service to Thekla in total loyalty, the youth knows he can never return to her father's service; what is total loyalty to one is total disloyalty to the other.

With Thekla's brief last farewell to her mother, the act ends.

Acts IV and V

Events thus far in *The Death of Wallenstein* have occurred in the second and third days of the four-day time analysis of the trilogy; Acts IV and V occupy the fourth day. The scene is now shifted from Pilsen to Eger, as a German audience would expect, much as an American audience might expect a Civil War play to end at Appomatox. To a non-German audience, the shift is hardly noticeable.

In IV, 1, Gordon, the commandant of the town, has the interesting minor role of a man persuaded to betray because he is too weak and scared to make a judgment of his own; his persuader is Buttler, whose revenge on Wallenstein has now become a harsh obsession. In V, 1, Buttler is seen, involved in the practical arrangements for the assassination, with the three murderers, Geraldin, Macdonald (pronounced MAC-doNald), and Deveroux, all of whom play the parts they played in actual history. By no accident these two scenes of repugnant betrayals, IV, 1 and V, 1, are placed on either side of the scene (IV, 2) in which the supreme loyalty of Max Piccolomini is matched by the supreme loyalty of Thekla. Wallenstein's conversation with the burgomaster of Eger in IV, 1 reviews the salient features of his character: his staunch will, his quick discernment of men, his shrewd intelligence—and his duplicity.

The Assassination of Wallenstein

The final scene of the trilogy (*The Death of Wallenstein*, V, 2) poses two dramatic problems: the restoration of Wallenstein to dignity in the eyes of the audience, so that his death will not seem like the mere removal of a distasteful character; and his offstage death itself, which can be anticlimactic.

Schiller handles the first of these problems very well. The scene opens with an eight-line speech of Wallenstein's to the Swedish Captain, in which the sellout to the enemy is quickly completed and in which we detect no qualms of conscience. But, as Countess Terzky comes in, Wallenstein inquires with concern for his daughter. His terse comment is: "Her grief will grow more gentle. She will weep." He bids the countess leave him, but she begs to stay. As he gazes pensively out the window, he says:

> "There is a busy movement in the heavens.
> The tower flag is whipped with wind, the clouds
> Sweep swiftly past, the sickle of the moon
> Wavers, and formless light darts through the
>   darkness.—
> No star is visible. That dull gleam yonder,
> The only one, is out of Cassiopeia,
> And over there stands Jupiter—but now
> The blackness of the stormy sky conceals him."

He wishes he could see the star Jupiter:

> "It is the star that shines upon my life.
> The sight has often given wondrous strength."

After a pause the countess remarks: "You will see him again"—meaning the star Jupiter, but her brother-in-law replies:

> "See him again? —O never, never. . . .
> He's gone— He's turned to dust."

And when the countess asks: "Whom do you mean?" he continues:

"He is the happy one. He has concluded.
For him there is no future any more,
Fate spins no further snares for him—his life
Lies spread out gleaming and without a fold
And no dark stain is left on it. . . .
He is beyond desire and fear. . . ."

Countess Terzky guesses that he speaks of Max Piccolomini, as indeed he does, the masculine pronoun (him) applying quite naturally in German grammar to both the star Jupiter and to Max. The loss of Max has meant more to Wallenstein than we had expected of this reticent man:

"The flower has now vanished from my life,

.   .   .

For he stood next to me like my own youth,
He made reality a dream to me,
Around the mean significance of things
He shed the golden fragrance of the dawn. . . ."

Gradually we perceive in his words an indirect confession of his own moral inferiority and, more surprisingly, the fact that he has no further will to live.

His companion in this final hour of his life is Countess Terzky, his sister-in-law, with no word said about the duchess. Though there is nothing whatsoever erotic about their talk, the intimacy shared at this moment would be more plausibly shared by husband and wife. Literary kinships again obtrude themselves, for here the two stand as modified forms of Macbeth and Lady Macbeth.

The subsequent dialogue between Wallenstein and Gordon, the commandant of Eger, opposes the former's intolerable condescension and the latter's contentment with a humble lot; it is like the conversation between the oak and the reed in La Fontaine's

fable. Seni's rushing in with warnings of disaster indicated in the stars, however, comes too pat. Here, as
elsewhere in the trilogy, it is hard to see how any
actor could make the role of Seni believable. When
Gordon and Seni both kneel to Wallenstein and im-
plore him to fear impending dangers, the effect is
awkward and contrived. Death is only minutes away
now and the dramatist is striving to create tension.
The principal actor must, on his side, give the impression of a weary man already spiritually dead and indif-
ferent to physical death, possibly vaguely expecting it
and welcoming it. His last words are:

> "I wish to go and sleep a long, long sleep.
> The strain of these last days has been extreme.
> See to it they do not wake me too soon."

The director must exploit the next stage directions
with taste and care: offstage trumpets announcing un-
identified arrivals, the sudden murder of the chamberlain in the near-darkness at stage rear, ". . . two doors
in succession are heard being smashed in. —Muffled
voices— Sound of weapons—then suddenly profound
silence."

The Conclusion

Upon the empty stage comes presently Countess
Terzky, carrying a lighted candle, somewhat too
patently in imitation of Lady Macbeth in the sleep-
walking scene. And somewhat too patently in imitation of Octavius Caesar's coming upon Cleopatra at
the close of Shakespeare's *Antony and Cleopatra*, she
is discovered by Octavio Piccolomini, to whom she
announces that she has taken poison and has but a few

minutes yet to live. The self-poisoning recalls both Lady Macbeth and Cleopatra. The downfall of the house of Wallenstein further recalls the extinction of the house of Atreus. At the last moment of the play a courier delivers a letter for Octavio Piccolomini; it bears the imperial seal and is addressed to *Prince* Piccolomini. (Octavio was hitherto *Count* Piccolomini.) Thus Octavio has his reward, but he has no son to inherit the title.

In describing the total trilogy as a dramatic myth about loyalty and betrayal, we do not suggest for a minute that the work preaches. On the contrary, the characters move unaware of any "message," and each has its own independent dramatic life. Nor is any ultimate cause cited for these actions. Within the play, many betrayals result from Wallenstein's betrayal of the emperor, but outside the play's scope the emperor had already betrayed his word to Wallenstein. The reasons for the emperor's betrayal recede, in turn, into the mystery of human life. Before our eyes the guilty and the guiltless perish equally, and in the end our sympathies go to Max, whereas around the figure of Octavio a faintly satanic aura develops, despite his steadfast adherence to law and to duty. From the total work there emerges what Aristotle would have called "a certain grandeur," and we have no hesitation about declaring the Wallenstein trilogy Schiller's greatest work and one of the great plays of the world.

Mary Stuart

A mere six days after the premiere of *The Death of Wallenstein* Schiller wrote Goethe about a new drama on the subject of Mary Stuart, saying that the work would begin with the announcement of the death sentence already passed on the heroine and would relegate her entire biography to the antecedent action. With such concentration on the last three days of Mary's life, he judged his subject well-suited to "the Euripidean method," which, let us emphasize, is contrary to "the Shakespearean method." Letters of June and July indicate that the scenario was then in the stage of detailed planning. The drama was composed between April, 1799, and June, 1800, and the premiere was given at the Weimar Theater on June 14, 1800.

History

When Henry VIII of England died in 1547, succession in the Tudor line seemed assured by a son and two daughters, with no need to have recourse to two grandnieces and a grandnephew. By 1558 the son, one daughter, and one grandniece had died without heirs and the surviving daughter had begun her famous reign (1558–1603) as Queen Elizabeth I. At her suggestion (in part), the surviving grandniece, Mary Stuart, married in 1565 the grandnephew, Henry Stuart, Lord Darnley (who was Mary's half cousin). That marriage, after beginning as a passionate attachment, turned atrociously bitter, and in 1567 Mary connived at her husband's murder. Meanwhile, in 1566, she had borne Darnley a son, the eventual King James VI of Scotland and King James I of England. Thus, as of 1567, all persons agreed that Mary Stuart had legitimate claim to the English throne. The question was: when? Catholics everywhere said: at once! and lamented that Protestant Elizabeth had already ruled "illegitimately" for nine years. Protestants said: when and if Elizabeth dies childless, and they entreated her to marry and produce heirs. But Elizabeth chose to remain the Virgin Queen.

When she was six years old Mary Stuart had been sent to France and betrothed to French Crown Prince Francis. At age fifteen she married the prince. At age sixteen her husband, upon the accidental death of his father, became king of France and Mary became queen of France. Three days before her eighteenth birthday she was a widow—and an unhappy supernumerary at the French court. Meanwhile her mother had died, the throne of Scotland awaited Mary's return, and to Scotland she went in 1561. Four years later she took her half cousin as second husband, doting on him at first and later loathing him—not without cause. When she lured him to his doom on the night of February 9 or the early morning of February 10, 1567, she was acting under the spell of passion for her lover, James Hepburn, Earl of Bothwell. Shortly after the murder, which was engineered by Bothwell, a hasty divorce was arranged between Bothwell and his wife, and on May 15, 1567, the arch-Catholic Mary Stuart was married to Bothwell in a Protestant ceremony.

Public opinion turned immediately hostile and triggered an armed rebellion. The newlyweds sought safety in Bothwell's strongest castle. Surrounded there, Bothwell jumped out a window and escaped alone on horseback, Mary following him directly, disguised as a boy. With a small improvised army they rashly set out from Castle Dunbar on June 14 to capture Edinburgh. Six miles outside that city they were met by Scottish lords whose troops displayed a white silk banner on which was painted the corpse of Darnley, with the infant James in an attitude of prayer beside it. Mary parleyed until she obtained the concession of Bothwell's riding away free, then surrendered to her own nobles. The six-mile ride into Edinburgh took four hours, with swelling mobs of men and women shouting "Burn the whore!" and with Mary frantically shouting that she would hang every last man of her captors.

For three days mobs raged before her prison in Edinburgh until her captors conveyed her to distant Lochleven Castle on a lake isle. There the queen gave birth to Bothwell's offspring, a daughter or a pair of twins—it is unclear which, for no child survived. Ten months later she escaped to assume command of six thousand soldiers advancing to seize Glasgow. When these troops met opposing troops commanded by her half brother, they were defeated, and when Mary saw defeat imminent, she sprang to horse and galloped away with a mere handful of attendants. For three days and three nights she rode, sleeping only fitfully on bare ground "with the owls." Reaching the seacoast on May 16, 1568, she wrote her "sister Queen,"

Elizabeth, that she would be her guest in England within a few hours, and having sent the letter, she boarded a little fishing smack, which took her across the dividing water into English Cumberland.

Elizabeth's first impulse was to receive her kindly, but political counsels prevailed, and she had Mary "detained." At that point, Mary Stuart was in her twenty-sixth year and Elizabeth Tudor was thirty-five. Nineteen years later, at the beginning of 1587, Mary was still being "detained."

The "detainee" was well-treated. Elizabeth, for all her parsimony, allowed her prisoner fifty servants, lavish comfort, and all the functionaries of a royal court. Even the jailers had to bow before Mary as a queen. In the not infrequent changes of place of detention, dozens of wagons were needed to transport the prisoner's belongings, including her spaniels, her aviary, and her dovecote. Under supervision, she was even allowed to ride to the hunt. She passed the time with embroidery work, with books, with the raising of flowers, yet she pined, grew stout and rheumatic, lost all her hair, and was obliged to wear a wig. Still she refused to sign a retraction of her claim to the English or to the Scottish crown. Because she declined to address her son as king, her presents to the child were returned. Her correspondence required two secretaries.

Always Mary was suspected of complicity in attempts on Elizabeth's life, but the plots, aimed at killing Elizabeth and installing the prisoner as queen of England, failed. At last the members of Elizabeth's Council, with Elizabeth's knowledge, engaged *agents provacateurs* to organize another plot, with Anthony Babington as its leader. The enciphered plans were smuggled in to Mary and Mary's enciphered acquiescence was smuggled out again. Then, with the deciphered evidence in their hands, the members of the Council brought Mary to trial at Fotheringay Castle in October, 1586, and shortly thereafter Parliament passed sentence of death upon her.

At this point Schiller opens his play.

Events of the last four months of Mary Stuart's life are here compressed into three days, February 6, 7, and 8, 1587, though the garden scene of Act III requires the summer season. Schiller expressly stated that the Mary of his play should be twenty-five years old and the Elizabeth no more than thirty. Thus, it is as though Mary's execution occurred within a few weeks after May 16, 1568, when she first set foot on English soil, and the nineteen-year confinement is ignored.

In all justice the drama is named for Mary Stuart, for she is the mainspring of all action, but two leading actresses are required. Indeed, one of the problems in mounting this work is to keep a balance between the two roles. Despite the best directors, one of them is likely to steal the show, as Karoline Jagemann did in the role of Elizabeth at the premiere, to Schiller's surprise.

On no account is this a play about a faded coquette and a youthful beauty. Nor should Mary be played sentimentally. Only the nurse (Jane Kennedy), Schiller said, feels sentiment for her, her fate being exclusively to experience vehement passions and to kindle vehement passions in others. Particularly in Act V, Scene 1, the director should have Greek tragedy in mind; the spectator there should be dry-eyed with Aristotelian fear so that he may clearly see the strength of will in Mary's final actions.

Foremost among the elaborate symmetries of this play is the distribution of scenes between the two leading roles. Act I is devoted exclusively to Mary; Acts II and IV exclusively to Elizabeth; Act III brings the two of them together—unhistorically; Act V, in two scenes, contrasts their separate fates. The significance of this symmetry will emerge from our analysis.

Act I

The barren room in Fotheringay Castle, which is the setting for Act I, is a visual symbol for Mary's spiritual privation in her imprisonment—and also a striking departure from the conventional palace interiors of most of Schiller's scenes hitherto. It is contrary to historical fact, as we have seen. The ransacking of the apartment, however, did occur, and more than once. While the ransacking proceeds we hear the argument between Mary's faithful nurse, Jane Kennedy, and her jailer, the spiteful Sir Amias Paulet, who both closely resemble their historical counterparts. Through the 141 lines of this dialogue, as through the next 237 lines in which Mary takes part, expository information is brought forth naturally and without wasting a word. The note of mortal danger is sounded in the recalling of the fates of would-be deliverers: the historical Duke of Norfolk who was beheaded, Parry and Babington, both historical commoners, who perished under public and prolonged tortures.

When Mary enters (at line 142), her first words are significantly: "Compose yourself!" Of Paulet she then requests, as the real Mary repeatedly did, an interview with Elizabeth, and also for the ministrations of a priest, which in real life she had until the last few hours before her death. But the churlish Paulet refuses or evades these requests.

With the entrance of Mortimer (at line 379), a sudden hope is raised for an eleventh-hour rescue, yet it is from this unexpected friend that Mary learns of the death sentence—news that Paulet hinted at but refused to reveal. Mortimer is Schiller's fictitious creation, but not out of whole cloth, a fair share of his traits having been drawn from Anthony Babington. Making him Paulet's nephew not only facilitated his entree into Mary's prison but also permitted typically Schillerian ironic play on the scores of loyalty and disloyalty, being and seeming-to-be. His secret conversion to Catholicism during a continental journey has about it that susceptibility to the glamor of Catholic ritual, without much concern for Catholic dogma, which constituted the "aesthetic Catholicism" popular in Germany around 1800.

At line 684 the wild new hope yields place to harsh despair in the person of Lord Burleigh, who now formally announces Mary's death sentence. Her spirited debate with him is almost as good stage argument as that between Wallenstein and Questenberg in *The Piccolominis*, Act II. We know that her cause is lost, but her defense is so lively that we are tempted to believe she could talk her way to safety, perhaps even to freedom, if she could but get to the proper authority. The real Mary talked much like this at her Fotheringay trial in October, 1586.

The act closes with a low-key discussion between Burleigh and Paulet, in which is given the assurance that the prisoner shall not be poisoned or in any other base way assassinated so long as Paulet is her jailer. Already this crusty Puritan has our respect.

Comprehensive and skillfully concise, the exposition has run to 1,076 lines, but it has been conveyed as vivid drama, not as narrative. Comparison with *The Piccolominis*, I, will reveal its mastery.

Act II

What we accepted, unaware of doing so, in Act I was the fact that all five characters each spoke his true feelings, even dissembling Mortimer, whom we there beheld in his genuine aspect. In Act II all is falsity. It is the morning of the second day, and we are in Elizabeth's palace of Westminster. The Earl of Kent is recounting to Sir William Davison the pretty details of an untrue war, a tournament where French mimic cannon fired bouquets at the fortress of the English queen's beauty and chastity. Elizabeth, entering with French and English nobles, protests untrue love for the Duc d'Anjou. The French deputies, who seek this loveless marriage only for diplomatic advantage, profess their own and their master's untrue affection and regard for her. Coyly Elizabeth evades the issue, and when she has sent them away empty-handed, she sounds out her English nobles with untrue humbleness. What is to be done about Mary Stuart? Burleigh honestly urges immediate execution; Shrewsbury honestly pleads for leniency; the Earl of Leicester dishonestly speaks such a farrago of flattery that we scarcely know what he does propose.

The discussion is interrupted by Sir Amias Paulet, who, true to his word, has delivered Mary's request for an interview, yet the honest man has in tow the dishonest Mortimer, his nephew, who is exploring opportunities for murdering Elizabeth. The debate is resumed: never grant the interview, says Burleigh; grant it by all means, says Shrewsbury; no one but the queen, says Leicester, can decide such a question.

But the queen cannot or will not decide. Instead, she sends her advisors away and detains Mortimer, who hopes to murder *her*, craftily proposing to him in veiled language that he murder Mary. Craftily he gives the impression of falling in with her plan. His uncle returns to fetch him, guessing with fair accuracy what must have gone on, but Mortimer assures him that assassination of Mary was never suggested.

Next, Leicester speaks privately with Mortimer, and schemer meets schemer. Briefly both masks are dropped as Mortimer delivers a letter from Mary to Leicester and Leicester admits that he loves the Scottish queen even as he pretends to languish after the English one. Shamelessly he confesses that he rejected a chance to marry Mary because marriage to Elizabeth offered greater advancement; now he is wasting his life for this capricious "Sultana." Mortimer's forthright proposal of liberating Mary immediately strikes lively terror in Leicester, so that when Mortimer is gone and Elizabeth comes back in, he suggests a stratagem: this very afternoon let Elizabeth go on a simulated hunting party, let her come "accidentally" to Fotheringay Park, and there let her grant Mary an interview "by chance." The scheme is to Elizabeth's taste; she will do just that—but if anything goes amiss, Leicester is to bear the blame! She languishes in false affection for him as the curtain falls.

The principals in this act are deceived deceivers and the watchwords here are lovelessness, guile, and untruth. We begin to discern the import of Schiller's play.

Act III

In history Elizabeth granted no interview, "accidentally" or otherwise, but the dramatist, in Aristotle's name, put poetic truth before historical truth by bringing the two women together, and audiences invariably support his practice.

Accompanied by Jane Kennedy and exulting in

freedom, Mary Stuart comes out into Fotheringay Park and, in seventy lines, speaks the most effective of Schiller's arialike passages, with little speeches by Jane Kennedy as sober interruptions. These green trees, Mary cries, provide a sweet illusion of freedom:

> "I rest upon the broad lap of the sky,
> Unfettered now and free, my eye
> Roves through its vast immensities.
> And yonder where the gray mist-mountains rise
> The borders of my realm advance,
> And yonder cloud that toward the south-land flies
> Is searching for the distant shores of France."

Suddenly comes Paulet, then Shrewsbury, proclaiming the imminent arrival of Elizabeth with Leicester and a hunting party. Mary is all in confusion as Elizabeth enters, asking "What castle is this?" and "Who is the Lady?" and showing calculated hostility before the prisoner's docile pleadings. So eager is Mary to please that she even offers—as the historical Mary never did—to renounce her claim to the English throne, but Elizabeth is bent on inflicting humiliation. Recriminations follow upon recriminations, until Elizabeth at last permits herself to say:

> "No one is anxious to be your—fourth husband,
> Because you kill your suitors as you kill
> Your husbands!"

The woman in Mary suddenly blazes forth as she replies:

> "I erred, but in a human, youthful way.
> I was seduced by power. I did not
> Conceal or make a secret of it. With
> A royal candor I disdained false seeming.

The world has known the worst of me, and I
Can say that I am better than my name.
But woe to you if from your deeds they once
Rip off the cloak of honor which you use
To hide the wild heat of your secret lusts.
It was not chastity your mother left you;
We all know what the virtue was for which
Anne Boleyn climbed the scaffold to the block."

The historical counterpart of this speech was a
letter Mary sent Elizabeth, in 1585, allegedly reporting
only what Mary had heard from the Countess of
Shrewsbury. It spoke of intimately reported anecdotes
of Elizabeth's vanity and vulgarity, then proceeded to
the running sore on Elizabeth's leg, suggesting congen-
ital syphilis, and to Elizabeth's paid lovers, culminating
in the report of Elizabeth's physical impediment to
marriage—what Ben Jonson told Drummond of Haw-
thornden was "a membrana on her which made her
incapable of man, though for her delight she tried
many."

In the play, as in history, the outburst sealed Mary's
doom. Schiller imposes restraint, but has Mary make
the generalized insults in the presence of Leicester and
the whole hunting retinue.

When Mortimer rushes to Mary in jubilation over
her "triumph," his excitement turns to passion and he
embraces her against her will. The shock value of such
lese majesty has worn off since 1800, but we imagine it
brought forth gasps in the court theater of Weimar.
The literary historian detects some degree of imitation
of a similarly shocking embrace in the final scene of
Goethe's *Tasso* of 1787.

Melodrama concludes Act III, first with the false
report that Elizabeth has just been assassinated outside
the park, then with the true report that an attempted

assassination has failed. In the play as in history, one further such attempt automatically required Mary Stuart's execution. Thus, Mortimer abandons Mary and flees, for even he now understands that all is lost.

Act IV

The two scenes of Act IV, an "Elizabeth act," portray the havoc wrought by Mary's outburst of truth upon Elizabeth's sphere of falsity. The French ambassador is expelled from England as an agent in attempted regicide. Burleigh so hints at Leicester's guilt in the afternoon's events that Leicester is in extreme alarm. When Mortimer comes to him with a well-intended warning, it suddenly occurs to him to save himself at the price of Mortimer's life. Instantly he calls the guards and bids them seize the youth as a traitor. Mortimer, in a gorgeous passage of melodrama, slays himself with a dagger before they can lay hands on him, his final cry being an invocation to Holy Mary wherein his fanatic's ecstasy blends Mary Stuart together with the Virgin Mary in heaven.

In IV, 2, Elizabeth is agreeing with Burleigh that his harsh policy alone was right, when Leicester comes with his artfully adapted version of Mortimer's death and regains primacy over Burleigh in Elizabeth's confidence. So eager is Leicester to exculpate himself now that he urges immediate execution of Mary Stuart, the woman he has claimed to love. With sly cruelty Elizabeth puts him in charge of that execution; then, to make doubly sure, she names Burleigh, his enemy, to share the responsibility.

In a fifty-nine-line soliloquy the queen opens her devious heart as she works herself up to the signing of the execution writ. Then she summons Sir William

Davison, gives him the signed document, but refuses to instruct him as to what he is to do. This seemingly implausible scene more precisely repeats historical fact than any other passage of the play. Davison's anguished cry of fear that he will be ruined, no matter whether he reveals or conceals the document, was only too well justified: the real Elizabeth sent him to the Tower for doing exactly what she wanted him to do.

The first of these two scenes offers a series of unmaskings of dissemblers. In the second, Leicester and Elizabeth, those two ruthless egotists, are driven to ultimate perfidy, the former to prolong for just a bit his admittedly loveless suit for the queen's hand, the latter to gain a brief delay of the public disclosure of her injustice. As Act V will show, both are thereby locking the gates of their private hells and throwing away the keys.

Act V

To the barren room of Act I the royal splendor is being restored, piece by piece, as the final act opens. The transformation betokens the change that has come over the captive herself since last we saw her. Such poetic use of the stage set is Schiller's new discovery, and nowhere does he manage it more effectively than here. In retrospect we realize that all five acts have had symbolic sets, even to the Rousseauistic relegation of palace interiors to the "bad" characters of Acts II and IV.

Mary's friends, as many of them as can get to her, gather around her: Jane Kennedy, her other ladies, her surgeon Burgoyne, and Melvil. In the most natural way in the world Margaret Kurl (the historical Elizabeth Curle) fetches a cup of wine to fortify the queen's spirits and sets it on the table. As the act proceeds, that inanimate object will undergo a poetic transformation to serve an important function later on.

Presently Mary enters, "magnificently dressed in white," her great black veil thrown back to reveal the diadem in her youthful hair; at her throat is an Agnus Dei, at her girdle a rosary, in her hand a crucifix. She is young, beautiful, strong, and serene. The Mary of history advanced slowly on rheumatism-swollen legs and in a costume that had required three hours to arrange. She wore a black velvet robe of state inset with gold and with a train so long that Sir James Melville had to carry it; a white veil wired to her wig fell all the way to her heels; her shoes were of soft white leather that would not creak; she wore the Agnus Dei at her throat, two rosaries at her girdle, and carried a crucifix. Thus, the grandly and stiffly posed Catholic martyr of history has yielded place to an angelic spirit about to rise to heaven.

The opening words of the stage Mary are: "Why are you weeping? Why are you lamenting?" and she goes on to bid all her friends rejoice, saying:

> "My prison opens, and my joyous soul
> On angel wings soars up to everlasting
> Liberty."

After farewells to many about her, she laments to Melvil that she is denied a priest and the sacrament. Whereupon Mevil discloses that he has been consecrated as a priest by the pope himself and that he has with him a gold case containing a consecrated Eucharistic wafer. The historical Sir James Melville, master of the household, was nothing of the sort, and the consecrated wafer in a gold case was in Mary's own possession. Her resident priest was that morning locked in his room to prevent his administering the "papistical" last sacrament.

The stage Melvil then points to that cup of wine Margaret Kurl had placed on the table, and we suddenly perceive that it is about to serve as a Communion chalice, spiritual refreshment for the queen and not mere physical refreshment. Modern stage lighting could impart a mystical glow to that chalice. But, alas, this is a Lutheran symbol, for in the Catholic rite of Schiller's time the priest alone drinks the wine, all others receiving the bread only. Schiller knew it was a Lutheran symbol, because in lines 3748-51 he has Melvil cite a papal dispensation for administering the Eucharist in both forms and even has him invoke an obscure ruling about "the priestly function of the kings of old," i.e., the right of monarchs to receive both the bread and the wine. Even before Melvil disclosed his secret priestly consecration, Mary mentioned the sacrament in terms of Matthew 18:20: ". . . where two or three are gathered together in my name . . . ," and she also likens herself to Saint Peter in Acts 12:6-10, where an angel delivered him from prison. These biblical allusions are not alien to the historical Mary Stuart, who, on the eve of her death, had solemnly eaten her last meal amid deliberate parallels to the Last Supper.

Before the administration of the Eucharist comes, necessarily, a last Confession. Dramatically, this obviates a self-revelatory soliloquy. Under solemn vow of truth and with death only minutes away, Mary confesses, in order, hatred of Elizabeth, sinful love of Leicester, guilt in Darnley's murder, and adultery with Bothwell, but she firmly denies any part in plots to assassinate the English queen. Melvil questions her sharply on this last point, but she insists she neither acted in or thought of such assassination. Here Schiller willfully exculpated his heroine, as the deciphered letters show. In what sense the stage Mary felt "sinful love" for Leicester is not clear; in any case it is nonhistorical. But Darnley's murder is crucial, and she truly confesses, "I caused the King, my husband, to be murdered." In Act I (lines 292–93) she had countered Jane Kennedy's argument that others had murdered Darnley with the words: "I knew of it. I let the deed be done,/ And lured him smiling to the toils of death." Her confession culminates in lines 3735–36:

> "God deems me worthy to atone for youthful grievous
> Blood-guilt by a death unmerited."

Schiller's subtle and noble conception is that Mary now accepts, indeed welcomes, her *illegal* execution *on the false charge* of attempted assassination as her *personal* atonement for her part in the murder of Darnley.

To this superb Confession scene, Schiller's random couplet-rhymes lend an awesome touch. The philosopher Herder, court chaplain at Weimar, protested, as did some others, that this scene constituted near-sacrilege, and early productions omitted it for that reason. Excerpted and translated into Russian verse, it was forbidden by the Russian censor. Moderns may well find it the poetic climax of the play.

The last remarks before Mary leaves to enter the scaffold chamber follow history closely, concluding with the lines:

> "My Saviour! My Redeemer!
> As on the Cross Thou didst spread wide Thy arms
> Of mercy, spread them to receive me now."

The Mary of history said: "Even as Thy arms, O Jesu Christ, were spread here upon the cross, so receive me into the arms of mercy, and forgive me all my sins. Amen."

Then, at the threshold, occurs the nonhistorical confrontation with Leicester; Mary's rebuke to him, mildly spoken but annihilating, is entirely of Schiller's invention. Excellent too is Leicester's thirty-seven-line soliloquy as he listens to the sounds coming from the execution hall but cannot summon the courage to watch. "She goes, already a transfigured spirit," he says, in further confirmation of the dramatist's idea of a troubled heart that has willed itself to atonement and to freedom. He hears "the Dean" exhorting her and her own voice praying; the real Dr. Fletcher prayed in English that God might lead false believers to the truth and the real Mary had prayed still louder in Latin. But Leicester himself rightly cries out like one already damned: "Hell's anguish seizes me!"

The brief V, 2 (fifty-seven lines) should be a twilight scene. To Elizabeth comes loyal Shrewsbury, reporting how Mary's secretary, in the Tower, is frantic with remorse for having testified falsely: his fellow secretary prompted him to it. Blandly Elizabeth agrees to reopen the case before it is too late. She sends for Davison in order to recall the execution warrant, and when he admits having turned it over to Burleigh, she rages at him (as she raged in history). When Burleigh arrives with the news she most wants to hear, she rages at him in turn. With feigned remorse she vows to be guided henceforth by none but Shrewsbury, the counselor of mercy and caution, but with unmistakable aversion he quits her service on the spot. She is then alone in the invisible prison of her vanity and untruth. But "love" is still left her. Of the Earl of Kent entering then, she asks that Leicester be sent to her. That lord, says Kent, "begs to be excused, he has set sail for France."

The Dramatic Myth

It is well known that Elizabeth I of England ruled prosperously for sixteen more years after 1587, presiding over an illustrious era and retaining her people's good will until her death, at age seventy, in 1603. She differed radically, therefore, from her stage counterpart in this play.

What Schiller did was to adapt a fraction of her personality and biography to make the negative force in a dramatic myth. From the personality and biography of the historical Mary Stuart he adapted a larger fraction to make the positive force in his dramatic myth. In both cases he freely added and subtracted details.

His Elizabeth is an epitome of egotism, hypocrisy, and cold lovelessness, using and destroying people for her own ends, though, like Octavio Piccolomini, she is often in the right and always on the side of law and order. She represents clever head over feeling heart, and is thereby Voltairean. Her suitor, Leicester, has the same negative qualities, with, however, enough heart in him to love genuinely elsewhere. His tragedy is to betray the better part of himself. Like Elizabeth, he commits murder by proxy and ends guilty, shunned, and alone, though tormented by a livelier conscience than hers.

Schiller's Mary is a passionate, spontaneous, Rousseauistic heart, freely giving affection and inspiring affection freely returned. To her guarded prison comes every last friend who can get in, and they weep genuinely for her. Mortimer dies for her sake. Her secretary is frantic with remorse for betraying her. Dead, she will be lovingly mourned, as Elizabeth, alive, is abandoned by all.

The two queens and, in gradations, the characters at levels below each, stand for love and lovelessness. All together enact a timeless dramatic myth about those fundamental qualities of human life.

The Maid of Orleans

Schiller's diary precisely dates the beginning of composition of *The Maid of Orleans* (*Die Jungfrau von Orleans*) as July 1, 1800—two weeks after the premiere of *Mary Stuart*—and its completion as April 16, 1801.

When Duke Charles Augustus learned that the new play dealt with Joan of Arc he was shocked. Was his theater to stage the comic-strip adventures of that silly whore, who, ever since Voltaire's poem *La Pucelle*, was the sniggering jest of all Europe? But when he discovered that this Joan of Arc was a very paragon of chastity, he was embarrassed by a wholly different problem. No actress in the Weimar troupe was thinkable in the role save Karoline Jagemann, and Karoline Jagemann was his own mistress. Because of the ducal embarrassment, the play was performed in Leipzig and Berlin before it reached the Weimar stage on April 23, 1803. Meanwhile the printed text, bearing the publisher's subtitle "A Romantic Tragedy," had been selling well since October, 1801.

From the outset the public delighted in the work, holding it in favor much above *Wallenstein* and *Mary Stuart* and quite disregarding the mockery heaped upon it by the Romanticists. For at least two generations its popularity continued, outranked in box-office receipts only by the phenomenal success of *William Tell* and the perennially welcome *Intrigue and Love*. Nor did admiration fail through the remainder of the nineteenth century.

History

Joan of Arc made her spectacular entrance upon the stage of history at the climax of the Hundred Years' War, and her brief action reversed the developments of some eighty years. Begun as a dynastic struggle between England and France, that episodic war had been initiated by Edward III of England in 1338. Its events form the background, from 1377 to 1422, for Shakespeare's historical plays, *Richard II*, the two parts of *Henry IV*, and *Henry V*. This last portrays the major English victory at Agincourt on October 25, 1415, after which the powerful Duke of Burgundy, who should have supported the French king, secretly concerted with the invaders to hold aloof from the conflict. By the Treaty of Troyes on May 21, 1420, Charles VI of France agreed to terms only a little short of surrender. His son, the dauphin, was disinherited; his daughter, Catherine, was to marry Henry V of England, and their yet unbegotten son was to rule both kingdoms. Charles VI himself, however, was to continue as king of France until his death.

The heir to the double kingdom, the future Henry VI, was born in December, 1421. In 1422 both ruling monarchs died, the French one elderly and infirm, the English one in the prime of manhood. Then English generals prosecuted the war in the name of the infant Henry VI, while the French generals Dunois and La

Hire continued to resist in the name of the disinherited dauphin. Amid the struggle, the dauphin, from
personal spite, murdered the Duke of Burgundy, with
the result that the infuriated Burgundians rallied to
their new duke and actively entered the war on the
English side. By 1428 the English had Paris and all of
northern France in their control, had crowned the six-
year-old Henry VI as king of the double kingdom,
and were besieging the dauphin's generals at Orleans.
For months the siege went on. Then, on April 29,
1429, Joan of Arc, a seventeen-year-old peasant girl,
assumed command of the French armies and within a
few weeks drove the English away from Orleans.

Born in Domremy, a hamlet in the province of Lorraine, in northeastern France, this illiterate girl had
pastured sheep, though her father seems to have been
one of the chief men of the village. She had three
older brothers and one older sister. While pasturing
her sheep, celestial voices, she said, specifically the
voices of Saint Michael the Archangel, Saint Margaret,
and Saint Catherine, had addressed her and bidden her
take up arms to save her country. A local nobleman,
Robert de Baudricourt, was at first astounded by her
claims, then wholly won over to her and to her mission. He and one of the girl's brothers accompanied
her to the dauphin's court, where that would-be monarch, skeptical but awed, gave her command of his
armies.

Reversal of the tides of war was almost immediate.
The English forces under Lord Talbot fled from Orleans, and in mid-June, at the town of Patay, suffered a
major defeat, though Talbot himself survived that
event by many years. By mid-July Joan had liberated
Rheims and seen her dauphin crowned there as King
Charles VII. In the struggle for Paris in September,
however, Joan was wounded. Through the slow win-

ter of 1429–30, many, including the newly crowned
king, began to doubt the divine authorization of her
mission. On May 23, 1430, she was captured near
Compiègne by a force of Burgundians, who quite
literally sold her to the Duke of Bedford and the English. Her one attempt at escape ended in recapture.
Meanwhile, her king made not the slightest effort to
ransom her or rescue her.

In January, 1431, she was transferred to a prison in
Rouen, the capital of English-held Normandy, and
there she was brought to trial before an ecclesiastical
court on charges of witchcraft and heresy. On May
30, 1431, she was burned alive in the marketplace of
Rouen. The inscription on her execution cap read:
"Apostate, schismatic, heretic, idolatress." She was
nineteen years old.

The war dragged on for another twenty years, and
ultimately the English lost all but minimal holdings on
the French coast. In 1455 the pope reviewed Joan's
trial, partly, it would seem, to affirm the legality of
Charles VII's coronation, and in 1456 the original ver-
dict was declared null and void. Some four and a half
centuries later, in 1920, she was canonized as Saint
Joan of Arc.

Voltaire's La Pucelle

Some three hundred years after her execution, Voltaire made Joan the titular heroine of a mock-epic
poem in twenty-one cantos, though she appears in less
than half the pages of that totally nonhistorical work.
As the genre required, there are scenes in heaven, in
hell, and on earth. The earthly ones are set near Orleans, with one long digression in Italy, perhaps because Voltaire was following the model of Ariosto's

Orlando Furioso. The primary supernatural characters are the French Saint Denis and the English Saint George, who bicker endlessly on earth as in heaven, until "the war" is finally settled in favor of the French saint.

As for Joan, she is here a sixteen-year-old stablemaid from a Domremy inn, offspring of a randy priest and a buxom chambermaid. Her flying donkey is actually one of her Domremy suitors in temporary asinine form (like Lucius in Apuleius's *Golden Ass*), but Saint Denis rides on a sunbeam. On one occasion she slights the good saint and the good saint is angry, but he is easygoing and in the end allows her to defeat Talbot and marry General Dunois. The coronation of Charles VII is mentioned only once as a future event, and all action is concentrated into a few weeks of 1429.

The story depends on the preservation of Joan's virginity as a magic charm, hence near-rape is her recurrent peril. In her closest call, Saint Denis imposes impotence on the Englishman John Chandos at the penultimate second, and Joan's magic is successfully preserved to the end. Other females, including nuns, regularly suffer the fate-worse-than-death. Agnes Sorel succumbs so many times that we lose count. All in all, *La Pucelle* is a one-joke story.

In 1800 one of Schiller's primary concerns was a literary "rescue," in Lessing's sense of that term; that is to say, the reinstatement to honor of a personage defamed by posterity and unable to defend himself from the grave.

Schiller's Play

In the stylized Prologue (432 lines), set in "a rural region," Joan is seen rejecting her father's plea that she marry the shepherd swain Raimond, as her sisters are now about to marry their respective suitors; to her, a divinely ordained mission of deliverance of her uncrowned dauphin is more important than marriage. To the group comes a local farmer named Bertrand. In his hands is a fine helmet mysteriously forced upon him by a gypsy woman at market. Joan begs to have the helmet, and when her father demurs, the gentle Raimond urges him to let her keep it. When all withdraw and leave Joan alone, she speaks a fifty-line monologue in rhymed stanzas, bidding adieu to her native regions and explaining how God spoke to her from amid the branches of a leafy tree, forbidding her the love of any man and directing her to rescue her king:

> "For when the bravest falter in the fight,
> When France is on the verge of last defeat,
> Then thou shalt hold My Oriflamme upright,
> And like the rapid mower in the wheat
> Put down the haughty conqueror in his might
> And give his fortune's wheel reverse complete.
> To sons of France thou shalt deliverance bring
> And set Rheims free and therein crown thy King."

The long Act I, in one continuous scene, presents the dauphin's court, Joan's arrival there, and her triumphant assumption of command over the French forces. The graceless Charles VII of history is here accorded good intentions, sensitivity, and a boyish helplessness. Agnes Sorel is his devoted mistress, whom dynastic considerations may debar from marriage but not from selfless love for him. She offers her jewels to set his finances in order once more. Around the dauphin are his loyal generals Dunois, known as the bastard of Orleans, and La Hire, as well as loyal courtiers. And the court is graced by a venerable paragon of an archbishop. A knight of Lorraine, named

Raoul, brings Joan in, explaining how a contingent of Lorrainers met the maiden, "beautiful yet terrifying to behold," near a forest and how she routed a superior force of the enemy by her mere glance. To Charles she promises his rightful kingdom and crown, from the archbishop she craves a blessing, but to the English herald she speaks the ringing defiance that closes the act.

Act II, again in one continuous scene, shows the enemy commanders in precipitate retreat from Orleans and wrangling over who is to blame for it. The dispute between the Englishmen Talbot and Lionel on one side and the renegade Duke of Burgundy on the other is settled by the renegade French Queen Isabeau, who detests no one so much as her son, the dauphin. This Isabeau is a female ruffian, brutal, forceful, and, as lines 1453ff. delicately hint, something of a nymphomaniac. On a cliff above the camp Joan appears with a party of French, and as they move down, their very presence inspires panic among the foe.

After line 1551 "the prospect opens. The English camp is visible in total flame"; which is to say that the midstage curtain is withdrawn, the burning camp is depicted on a painted backdrop, and we view "another part of the battlefield."

"After a time" the Welsh lad Montgomery enters, wandering in terror by himself after the rout, and chances upon Joan, also by herself. For heightened solemnity the pentameter verse yields to hexameters as the hapless lad throws himself on his knees and begs abjectly for his life, but Joan, like an implacable Valkyrie, slays him without pity. Invoking the heavenly Virgin, she declares her sword "moves of itself, as though it were a thing alive." Directly afterward she encounters the renegade Duke of Burgundy, and by her heartfelt rhetoric she persuades him to return to his duty and fight for France.

Act III, Scene 1 presents Charles's jubilant court as everyone lavishes praise and affection on Joan. In faintly comic rivalry, Generals Dunois and La Hire both sue for her hand in marriage. Both the dauphin and Agnes Sorel would like to assist in this charming dilemma, but Joan rejects their services as she rejects both suitors, solemnly warning them all of grave events still impending.

Act III, Scene 2 takes us to the mortally wounded English General Talbot on the battlefield. That he is a gallant yet formidable enemy we have already seen, but now we see him in typically Schillerian antithesis to Joan's submissive faith. Talbot is a man of reason, a man of the limited Voltairean-type intellect, a man of religious disbelief. Aware that he is dying, he cries out:

> "Inanity, you win, and I must perish!
> With stupidity the gods themselves contend
> In vain. Sublimest Reason, light-clear daughter
> Sprung from the godhead's brow, wise founder of
> The universe, directress of the stars,
> Who are you, if, tied to the horse's tail
> Of Idiocy, that frenzied steed, and crying
> With helpless cries, you see yourself paired with
> The drunken and hurled down to the abyss!
> A curse on any man who turns his life
> To great and worthy things and with wise spirit
> Devises well-laid plans! The King of Fools
> Is winner of the world."

And when Lionel has regretfully left him to go back into battle, Talbot speaks his final words as a soliloquy:

> "Soon all will end, and I to earth give back,
> And to the everlasting sun, the atoms
> That were conjoined in me for joy and sorrow,—

And of the mighty Talbot who had filled
The world with warrior's fame, there will be nothing
Left but a handful of light dust. —Such is
The end of man. —and as for profit, all
We gain out of the struggle of our lives
Is insight into nothingness, and cordial
Contempt for everything that once had seemed
Sublime to us and worth the wishing for."

For Talbot, the atheist and the materialist, "death closes all"; his end contrasts with Joan's death at the end of the play, among friends and with "the heavens opened."

Up as far as this III, 2, historical events have been followed, however vaguely, in this play, but beginning with the nonhistorical death of Talbot everything else in the scenario is almost totally fictional and of Schiller's contriving.

Act III, Scene 3, with its mere 116 lines, brings us to the turning point of the play and offers difficulties in interpretation, difficulties that we believe were deliberate on Schiller's part.

Within sight of Rheims, the coronation city, a Black Knight obtrudes himself into Joan's path. From inside the black armor a voice recalls her mission to see her king crowned in Rheims, but bids her advance no further, lest she perish. Her blow aimed at this adversary is stayed by a mere touch of the Black Knight's hand; "Kill something that is mortal," says his voice. Then, amid lightning and thunder the apparition sinks into the ground. In lines 2422–25 the phantom had said:

"Let thus much fame achieved suffice you and
Dismiss the Fortune [*das Glück*] that has served you
    like
A slave, before it frees itself in anger;
It hates faith and serves no one to the last."

This much-debated passage, which sounds like an angry jinn from an Arabian Nights tale, may suggest a parallel with the death of Moses within sight of the promised land (Deuteronomy 34:4) or, more likely, the notion of Greek *moira*, that predetermined maximum of one's achievement. We suggest a "dark power in human life" whose nature is a grudging envy of achievement. In any case, Schiller assigned no allegorical label.

A mere eight lines later, Joan is challenged to combat by the Englishman Lionel. She defeats him, but as she wrenches open his helmet to slay him, as she has slain so many others, she is suddenly smitten by the human desire for a man's love and she cannot kill him. She even begs him to kill *her*, which he refuses to do. But he takes her sword as a token that he will seek her out again—in love.

Here, all in a moment, Joan plummets from God's elect to mortal womanhood. One impulse of desire and she is undone. The "divinity" thrust upon her by God was none of her choosing, yet by shirking that "divinity" even for a moment she "sins," she falls. In Schiller's scale of values, she *unnaturally* negated womanliness when she assumed the divine charge, and now a momentary lapse into womanliness destroys her.

Out from the coronation ceremonies she comes fleeing from her own oppressive guilt into Rheims cathedral square—the "short stage"—and there she is happy to encounter her sisters and friends from Domremy. But then her stern father steps up and denounces her as an impure girl, as a false saint, as a witch. Bowed under her sense of guilt she cannot reply. Peals of thunder seem to confirm the accusations, and by the end of the act everyone has abandoned her and denied her—except the gentle Raimond. Meanwhile (at line 2761) the midstage curtain was drawn to permit the use of the "long stage" in the elaborate coronation procession.

In V, 1 Joan is recognized as "the witch of Orleans" even by charcoal burners in a deep forest, but to the faithful Raimond she denies all witchcraft and bows to God's will in all things, even in these false accusations. Just then, through the woods, comes the wicked queen Isabeau with a party of English. Exultantly she takes Joan captive, sending her, against urgent pleadings, to Lionel. In V, 2 Raimond brings news of this capture to Joan's friends, who have begun to have second thoughts about abandoning her.

In V, 3 Joan is captive in a watchtower, where Lionel, from distinctly earthly love, is fending off a mob who would tear her to pieces. As a French force moves against the tower, Lionel goes out to battle, leaving Isabeau to guard the prisoner. As the English forces close in, Isabeau raises a dagger to slay the chained girl, but Joan kneels in prayer. At the sound of the cry "The king is captured!" she is vouchsafed the strength of Samson to break her chains, overpower the nearest soldier, and escape. Isabeau stands stupefied. To the victorious La Hire as he enters, Isabeau surrenders her sword and asks to be taken to any place where she will not confront the dauphin, her son.

The forty lines of V, 4 comprise a battlefield tableau, with Joan mortally wounded and lying unconscious in the arms of her friends. The wind is whipping dozens of flags at stage rear. Sunset light is over all. Joan rouses. She is given her own flag, which she had abandoned in the coronation cathedral and which she says she must lay down before the throne of God. Her nine concluding lines exclaim upon the rainbow in the air and upon the Madonna, glimpsed amid choirs of angels at the golden gates of heaven; then she speaks of her "assumption":

"Light clouds bear me up.—
My heavy armor has become winged raiment.
Upwards—upwards. —Earth is rushing back.—
Brief is the pain, and joy is everlasting."

Her flag slips from her grasp in sign of death. The king gestures for all the flags to be laid down over her. A slow curtain descends as flag after swirling flag is brought forward and floats down, shedding a profusion of colors over her lifeless form.

With these lines we reach the climax of a development in Schiller himself. *Don Carlos* ended in despair and blackness. The *Wallenstein* trilogy ended, literally and figuratively, in the first gray of dawn. Mary Stuart's last speech included the words:

". . . I am on the path departing
From this world to become a blessed spirit . . ."

and Melvil, in lines 3754–57, had already said to her:

". . . yonder in His kingdom of pure joy,
Where there is no more sin and no more weeping,
You will, as a transfigured angel,
Be joined with God in His eternal keeping."

Now the dying Joan beholds the heavens opened and her joyous spirit ascending toward glorious light.

Problems

Defining *The Maid of Orleans* as a dramatized saint's legend, the work should be visualized by a reader or a director as a sun-flooded cathedral window sprung into life. Its religiosity, however, is spurious, and we do well in recalling that its author was nominally a Protestant, that in his early plays, as we have noted, he displayed anti-Catholic sentiments, and that in his mature years he was an idealistic freethinker. Why, then, it will be asked, did he so enthusiastically compose a play dealing with a Catholic saint's legend? The answer is that he was emulating the new literary fashion set by the German Romanticists.

The play was both a response and a challenge to Ludwig Tieck's enormously long book-drama, *Genoveva* (1799; published, 1800). This dialogized narrative about Saint Genevieve, the patron saint of Paris, so transfigured eighth-century Catholicism from what it had been in reality, so poetized it with sensuous beauties, that a wave of conversions to Catholicism resulted—until the public became aware that its author was a nonconformist Lutheran. Schiller, too, was impressed by this work, which sought to synthesize Shakespeare with Calderón. It offered new material. It was a challenge. Inevitably he designed his own medieval saint's legend as a workable theater piece, thereby 'automatically contesting *Genoveva* by seeming to correct it. By attempting *any* medieval theme he was invading the preserve of the *Romantiker*, who, by definition, were Romantic medievalists, and the *Romantiker*, since 1798 and even before, had been markedly antipathetic to Schiller, who, in Anglo-Saxon terms, would be termed a Romantic Hellenist. In short, we are confronted here with an abstruse quarrel of literary ideologies. Suffice it to say that the *Romantiker* heaped mockery upon *The Maid of Orleans*, that the general public flocked to performances of the work long after *Genoveva* had lost favor, and that both works have their values. Of the two, Schiller's play was and is accessible to many more people than the other, yet a modern literary connoisseur may not be blamed for preferring the eccentric originality of Tieck. One of the "problems" with *The Maid of Orleans* is the fact that it exploited a transitory fashion.

The nationalistic component of the play is a debatable one. A major theme, certainly, is the expulsion of English invaders from the French homeland, but the play is by a German writer. When, after 1805, Napoleon took over central Europe, he banned the work because, with substituted nationalities, it could be interpreted as a parable against his invasion and takeover.

Schiller's foremost attention, however, was concentrated on the mythic values of the play. On the one hand, Joan's faith is opposed to Talbot's non-faith, while on the other hand, Joan's purity is opposed to the gross sensuality of the harridan Isabeau. This double-strand myth may be set parallel to the single-strand myth of the loving and the loveless, which was the essence of *Mary Stuart*.

As we saw, the general notion of Joan of Arc prior to 1800 derived from the totally nonhistorical and scurrilous poem by Voltaire. Before that poem, only one literary treatment is known. Under the name of Shakespeare there appears in the First Folio of 1623 the play of *Henry VI*, in three parts and with a total of fifteen acts, and in Part I Joan appears as one of the characters. Portrayal of her there is inconsistent, since in the early acts she seems to be a benign character performing her military mission at the behest of the Mother of God, but in the later acts she conjures fiends from hell (who sullenly refuse to do her bidding) and then denies any association with fiends. She is burned by the English, with no mention of an ecclesiastical trial, as a witch. She is also shown to be sexually promiscuous and a brazen liar. It is charitably supposed that Shakespeare, at the outset of his career

around 1590, did no more than revise this play of unknown authorship but dated to the 1580s.

From this work, Schiller may have borrowed a few
hints but no more. His primary concern was with a
reversal of the defamatory notion of Joan purveyed
by Voltaire. Such was the international fame of *The
Maid of Orleans*, however, that investigations of the
historical Joan were undertaken. Ironically, these have
not only disproved Shakespeare's revision and Voltaire's poem, but Schiller's play as well. Still more
ironically, the researches have resulted in radically
divergent views so that the conclusions are, to this
day, highly controversial.

To the French historian Jules Michelet (before
1846) Joan was the embodiment of the French national character, with emphasis on common sense (*le
bon sens*), and of a decidedly nineteenth-century
patriotism. According to Bernard Shaw, the portrayal
of Joan in Shakespeare's *Henry VI*, Part I, "may be
dismissed as rubbish"; Voltaire's ribald irreverence
may be "more wholesome than the beglamored sentimentality of Schiller," whereas Schiller's play itself is
"a witch's caldron of raging romance." Mark Twain
portrayed Joan as "an unimpeachable American school
teacher in armor" and clad her "with as many petti-
coats as Noah's wife in a toy ark." Anatole France's
biography reduced Joan absurdly to the status of a
mere mascot for General Dunois. The Scotsman An-
drew Lang made her into a military leader of genius,
while stoutly insisting on her physical beauty and her
perfect Victorian modesty. Shaw himself stressed the
point that Joan's fellow soldiers found her repug-
nantly unattractive. In 1920 the Catholic Church
canonized Joan as an authentic saint in the strictest
traditional sense. Out of the general controversy
emerged Shaw's own play, *Saint Joan* (1923), and its

preface (1924). In the former, Joan is a tragic figure, though with comic aspects; by taking her orders directly from Saint Michael the Archangel, Saint Margaret, and Saint Catherine, she bypassed pope and church and anticipated Protestant principles; by championing Frenchmen of all social classes, she disrupted the "horizontal" structure of society whereby the international aristocracies were opposed to the lower social strata of any country. Thus, Joan was a Protestant before Protestantism and a nationalist before nationalism and both things determined her ruin. As for the celestial voices, those, says Shaw, will be readily seen as Francis Galton's "visualizations," and as for Joan's choice of death above recantation, that was "a Rationalism carried to its ultimate test of suicide."

Shaw's play and preface together compose the modern skeptic's perfect guide to Joan's life and times. In 1921, however, Dr. Margaret Murray had set forth an anthropological explanation of Joan in *The Witch-Cult in Western Europe*, and in 1933 offered further evidence in *The God of the Witches*. Opposing witch "diagnoses" by folklorists, psychologists, and fanciful occultists alike, and insisting on anthropological methods, Dr. Murray finds Joan to have been a witch —as the ecclesiastical tribunal of 1431 said—which is to say she was a member of an organized and very ancient witch religion that practiced fertility rites concurrently with Christianity down to its dissolution in the eighteenth century and the era of the widespread and sensational witch trials. Bizarre as this interpretation seems at first glance, Dr. Murray not only provided much evidence for her claims but she also offered startling new interpretations for factors—such as the voices—that other writers have passed over.

The upshot of all this is that Schiller's play, insofar as it professes to deal with Joan of Arc, is as unacceptable to thoughtful moderns as Voltaire's poem. If, as someone has suggested, Schiller had only written his play about Snow White, he could have had his pure maiden, his harridan queen, his visual spectacle, perhaps even his atheist-materialist Talbot, and certainly his lofty dramatic myth, and we would all admire his work. There is about the play as a whole the quality of a fairy tale, and a splendidly dramatized fairy tale. But to thoughtful moderns, Joan of Arc as the heroine of a fairy tale is unthinkable.

People less concerned about the historical Joan will raise other objections. A post-Freudian looks askance at the warrior maiden on whom virginity confers physical strength. The Women's Rights movement may take inspiration from the Joan of history but not from the poetic one. The "good" characters at the French court now seem mawkish. The play as a whole seems to moderns generally to be lost in a bygone era.

Nor is it possible to put the blame on the present harsh and discordant generation or to suppose that shifting tides of taste will sooner or later float this play back into favor. The intellectual substructure of the work has collapsed. It is false to Joan, it is false to medieval history, it is psychologically false to human nature. More's the pity! because *The Maid of Orleans* is a superbly stageworthy piece.

The Bride of Messina

After completing *The Maid of Orleans* in April, 1801, Schiller somewhat abated his headlong pace of composition, though he contemplated various dramatic themes in the course of the ensuing fourteen months or so. What he actually settled down to write in the late summer of 1802 was his long-contemplated "Rival Brothers," which now received the title *The Bride of Messina, or The Hostile Brothers* (*Die Braut von Messina, oder Die feindlichen Brüder*). Within six months it was completed, on February 1, 1803. Goethe immediately put it into rehearsal and the highly successful Weimar premiere was given on March 19. Published in June, the text sold six thousand copies before Schiller's death in 1805.

The theme of two brothers quarreling over a girl to the point of fratricide harks back to that pair of storm-and-stress plays of 1776, Leisewitz's *Julius of Taranto* and Klinger's *The Twins*, from which a major strand of *The Robbers* was drawn. All three works had rival brothers and a suffering father, but no mothers were in evidence. In the new work the father is recently deceased and the mother is the dominating figure, perhaps in compensation for the lack of mothers in Schiller's plays to date. There had been only two: the vapid Mrs. Miller, who unaccountably dropped out of the story in *Intrigue and Love*, and Wallenstein's all but superfluous duchess. The girl in the new work is a sister, though neither she nor her brothers are aware of the kinship. The four members of this family live apart, with an old retainer as go-between, so that the cast consists of only five characters, not counting two unnamed messengers. Each brother, however, is accompanied by a retinue of twelve warriors, who function as a modified form of the ancient Greek chorus. We recall that the plan for "The Knights of Malta" included a Greek-type chorus of warriors. Here, some of these soldiers must do double duty as the mute chorus of city elders in the opening scene. The action is set in the Sicilian city of Messina at a date about 1060.

Strictly speaking, there *is* no history in *The Bride of Messina*, the scenario being wholly of Schiller's invention and a means of escaping from history. Yet certain historical data were selected and rearranged to make the scenario. These data concern those Northmen out of Sweden who, in 911, established themselves athwart the lower Seine and in time became the Norman French. Even before their duke invaded and conquered England in 1066, the Hauteville family, father and several sons, seized territories in far-off Italy. From Naples southward their power grew until, in 1060, Count Roger I began a thirty-year conquest of Sicily. After 1130 his son, Roger II, assumed the title of King of Sicily and Italy and ruled, from Palermo, over a population divided among three religions—Roman Catholic, Greek Orthodox Catholic, and Moslem—and speaking four different languages—French, Italian, Greek, and Arabic. Messina, always an important port city, was never the capital. In Palermo, however, two widowed queens ruled briefly, Queen Sibyl for a few months in 1194 and Empress Constance for about a year, 1197–98. The latter might well interest a German writer, since she was the mother of Frederick II, the greatest of German emperors, and in her own right an uncommonly interesting personage.

Schiller postulates an island kingdom of mixed and antagonistic populations, a ruling family precariously in control of conquered inhabitants, and a capital city, Messina, which is familiar with three religions, though he gives the impression that the Greek elements are those of classical antiquity. The characters bear an odd assortment of names drawn from Spanish, general Romance, and Germanic.

The Characters

The characters are not dramatic personalities like those in Schiller's other plays, but human types in stylized poses. They are "monolithic." They neither evolve nor vary, nor were they meant to.

The hostile brothers, Don Manuel and Don Cesar are young warrior princes, intrepid, proud, defiant, strong. Don Manuel, as the older, tends to be thoughtful and prudent; Don Cesar, as the younger, is given to rashness and impetuosity. Otherwise they are twinlike. The old retainer Diego is an old retainer and nothing more—except a dramatic convenience. The two unnamed messengers are not even listed as part of the cast. Isabella, the mother of the two princes, is their mother and little more. She grieves at their quarrels, she exults in their reconciliation, she is crushed by their deaths. Only in Act IV (lines 2360ff.) is she particularized by a rash and defiant atheism:

> "The art of seers is emptiness of sight,
> They are deceivers or they are deceived, . . ."

and a few lines later:

> "Good-natured, simple fools, what do we gain
> By all our faith? It is impossible
> To reach the gods who dwell on high, just as
> One cannot shoot an arrow to the moon."

Here we catch echoes of sentiments two or three times expressed by Jocasta in Sophocles's *Oedipus the King* and we perceive that Isabella is partly modeled on Jocasta. We note further that the potential brother-sister incest is Schiller's substitute for the actual mother-son incest of *Oedipus*, and that the two messengers, of lines 535ff. and 2117ff., parallel the two shepherds who deliver crucial information in the ancient play. The Greek chorus is imitated, in part, from the same classical source, but also in part from Euripides's *Hippolytus*, while the opening and closing scenes are Schiller's thoughtful "modern" equivalents of the corresponding parts of the *Hippolytus*. Thus, the play as a whole blends elements from Leisewitz and Klinger with elements—especially formal elements—from Sophocles and Euripides.

The daughter and sister, Beatrice (pronounced Bay-ah-TREET-say) is a sentimental girl straight out of storm-and-stress.

The Scenario

The play begins superbly with Isabella's one hundred-line address to the elders of Messina, but, where Euripides allowed the goddess Aphrodite to ap-

pear alone on stage and speak a long narrative prologue, Schiller felt bound to make his opening scene
dramatic. Thus, Isabella's narrative address is delivered
by her, as queen, to a chorus of elders, who hear her in
silence and then "withdraw with their hands on their
hearts." Isabella announces that she has sent for her
quarreling sons, that she may reconcile them, and her
final line hints at the hubris in her character as she
suggests that the elders will have to accept their new
prince whether they like him or not.

Isabella then despatches Diego to fetch her daughter
from the convent where she has long been concealed.
At line 131, her two sons arrive, each with his twelve-
man retinue. Their mother pleads with them. Before
our eyes the two are reconciled, but not before a messenger comes to Don Cesar with the report that a
certain lost lady has been found. Don Cesar leaves at
once to look into the matter. Then Don Manuel, addressing his own warrior band, relates how for five
months he has secretly courted a girl whom he discovered during a hunting expedition—a fugitive white
doe led him to her—and how he intends this very day
to reveal his identity to her, marry her, and make her
the princess of Messina. Chorus speeches of a total of
120 lines conclude Act I on the same lofty tone on
which it opened.

In a seaside garden (II, 1) Beatrice, while waiting
for Don Manuel, her secret lover, voices doubts about
her own conduct in a long operatic-type *scena*. She is
troubled not only by five months of nocturnal trysts
but also by her secret attendance at her father's funeral. Unaware that the deceased ruler was her father,
she had gone from curiosity and idle whim, and there
she had been importuned by Don Cesar in disguise.
His men have discovered her and brought her this
very day to this castle and garden, and she left her

convent willingly because she believed them to be Don Manuel's men. To her horror, Don Cesar now arrives. She flees into the garden house and Don Cesar's men guard the door. At the palace (II, 2), Don Manuel acquires enough information to allow him to deduce that his beloved is his sister. He hurries to her (Act III), but their garden colloquy is surprised by Don Cesar, who murders his brother on the spot. His final order to his men is to convey the swooning girl to his mother at the palace.

Act IV discloses the individual and collective guilt of all parties. Don Cesar, overwhelmed by remorse, is temporarily dissuaded from suicide by his mother and sister, but his indecision is abruptly resolved by a stunning invention of Schiller's.

An offstage choir is heard singing. The great double doors at stage rear open to reveal the palace chapel and the scaffolding supporting Don Manuel's coffin above its empty grave. Beholding that sight, Don Cesar plunges a dagger into his heart and throws himself at Beatrice's feet. She, however, turns away into her mother's embrace. The chorus concludes the work with the lines:

> "Of all possessions life is not the highest,
> The worst of evils is, however, *guilt*."

In this finale of somber pomp—chapel, candles, choral music, coffin, and open grave—we see the ingenious "modern" equivalent of those awesome epiphanies with which Euripides, but not Sophocles frequently concluded his dramas.

The Adaptation of Greek Form

The Bride of Messina, be it noted, approximates a Greek play, but not a Greek performance. It was designed for the theater of 1803, with its footlights, curtain, wings, and backdrops, not for presentation on an Athenian April morning under religious auspices. Its 2,842 lines may be compared with the 1,530 of *Oedipus the King* and the 1,466 of *Hippolytus*. It strictly observes the Unities of Time and Action, but the Unity of Place—which Aristotle never mentioned—is modified to permit scenes in and near Messina. Originally, these scenes were intended for uninterrupted performance, by means of using the midstage curtain, and were symmetrically disposed in five "acts," as follows:

1. a colonnaded hall in the palace of Messina; 981 lines; deep stage
2. a seaside garden outside the city; 279 lines; shallow stage with painted midstage curtain
3. "a room in the palace;" 447 lines; deep stage
4. the seaside garden, as before; 322 lines
5. the colonnaded hall again; 813 lines; backstage extension revealed

For reasons not clear to us, Schiller then chose to blur his own symmetry by combining 2) and 3) into the two scenes of Act II, so that the total work now appears in four acts.

No divinities appear. The characters are all mortal, as in the works of Corneille, of Racine, and in Goethe's *Iphigenia in Tauris*. But in showing both a murder and a suicide on stage, Schiller broke the dramatic taboos of Athens and Versailles alike.

The chorus is a double one, twelve and twelve, in contrast to the ancient chorus, which probably had fifteen members, plus a chorus leader. (Schiller may have taken a cue from lines 58–120 of *Hippolytus*, where a second chorus appeared, though this point is debated by scholars.) Schiller put his two groups of twelve on stage, with no attempt to create an equivalent of the ancient "dancing circle" (orchestra), and he motivated their comings and goings and set them in dramatic opposition. March music accompanies their simultaneous entrance after line 131, but thereafter no music is used. Schiller never intended them to sing. He did wish, originally, that they should speak in unison, but when such voice choirs proved too cumbersome, he portioned out his "odes" among individuals, to whom he then, for convenience's sake, assigned names.

The two groups of twelve consist of "old knights" and "young knights," respectively. Their military costumes, as of a nonexistent kingdom about 1060, will require tact, but the two sets must sharply contrast with each other and must, together, be visually effective. The stage direction after line 131 says merely that each group is "distinguished by its own colors and emblems." No flags are mentioned, but two in each group could be used for good effect. Spectacle is an important ingredient of the play and these twenty-four men provide the color and movement.

No ballet dances are needed, but a choreographer is indispensable. When, after line 2,429, the First Chorus "disperses before [Don Cesar] in movements of flight," twelve men must move to predetermined points and for a predetermined number of seconds hold postures indicative of stylized running, as though in horror. Three lines later, they must pivot and return to points from which each can view the corpse of Don Manuel. The same twenty-four men must speak almost eight hundred lines, or twenty-eight percent of the text. If voice choirs are practicable, well and good; if not, the speeches had best be parceled out as they now appear in the printed text. Better twenty-two, or even twenty, supple bodies in coordinated motion with two, or four, articulate speakers, than twenty-four mumblers who dance or twenty-four sonorous reciters who shuffle.

Their poetry is expressive in its dramatic context, where, like the ancient chorus, it voices, within a suspension of time, the thoughts of soberly judging mankind. Over Don Manuel's body, Berengar says, for instance, at the end of Act III:

> "Out of the sun-illumined earth
> As easily fades an action's trace
> As facile expression fades from a face.
> Yet nothing is lost or disappears
> Once the mysterious ordaining years
> Have taken it into their darkling womb.
> Time is a meadow in ageless bloom,
> Nature is a living thing indeed,
> And all things are fruit and all things are seed."

The Play as a Whole

Read or acted realistically, *The Bride of Messina* turns to nonsense; properly understood and properly presented, it is a unique "ballet with words" and very moving. Production must begin with the colors. With these in mind, the dance steps and miming gestures must be practiced under an imaginative choreographer and coordinated with the choral recitations. Only then will it be time to introduce the actors. These must be directed as the leading "dancers" in this unique corps de ballet. Their movements and poses must be stylized, and the five personages, in their stylized costumes, must emerge from the choruses as a conspicuous appliquéd design "emerges" from a rich cloth. Particular care needs to be taken with Beatrice, that girl strayed out of a sentimental tableau by Greuze into a painting by Rembrandt.

It might be wise to rethink the matter of the stage décors. That colonnaded hall is incongruously neoclassical, that seaside garden with its garden house is incongruously rococo. With modern lighting and with imaginative use of curtains, these sets might be eliminated altogether, to the facilitation of realizing Schiller's very good original intention of continuous action.

Let Don Manuel's murder be a ballet-murder, and let Don Cesar's suicide be a ballet-suicide, but let the revelation of that palace chapel convey, with all the resources of modern machinery, the horror of an open and waiting grave. This is a Fate tragedy, true; but it is also a kind of horror play. The director will need all the ingenuity possible to avoid making that chapel look like a funeral parlor. Perhaps his ingenuity could transform that static revelation at stage rear into some kind of dynamic movement that engulfs Don Cesar. This is, after all, the modern equivalent of a Euripidean epiphany, and it should be overwhelming.

Yet the very last impression should be a full silence out of which come the final five lines of the hushed chorus, closing with: "The worst of evils is, however, *guilt*."

at the cast-of-characters page will show that the three cantons are represented by seven persons each. The accurate and complex geography of the play indicates that Schiller worked with a map before him.

The traditional five-act organization is retained, but these are subdivided into scenes, a total of fifteen. In II, 1 and in IV, 2, we see the interior of Baron von Attinghausen's Gothic hall, idealized in its patriarchal simplicity, and in the second-last scene of the play we see the interior of Tell's house. The remaining twelve scenes are out of doors, now on the shores of the lake, now in a town square, amid a forest or in a meadow, along a picturesque road or in a picturesque grove. All of these required elaborate painted sets, the most spectacular being the moonlit II, 2, where the confederates meet in a mountain meadow on the Rütli, beneath a view of ice-capped peaks, descending down past glaciers to the eastern end of the lake. In 1804 such scenes were dazzling novelties, a picture book come to life.

For authentic details Schiller relied on travel books and on Goethe's recollections from two Swiss journeys, in 1775 and 1797. Thus, the text, in addition to its complex and specific geography, is dotted with bits of local color: an occasional word of Swiss dialect, names with the characteristic ending in *i*, the chamois and the chamois hunter, the mountain winds and the abrupt and dangerous lake storms, and those "melodious tones of cowbells" heard offstage before and after the rise of the curtain on Act I. When the countrymen affectionately discuss their milch cows by name—such as "brown Liesel"—we realize with a start how far we have come from Racinian decorum. Even Lady Milford's drawing room seems to belong to another lifetime.

In the matter of the Unity of Action, Schiller has brought to pass a small miracle. Many story strands

William Tell

While at work on *The Maid of Orleans* in 1801 Schiller was startled to hear of a rumor that he was composing a play about William Tell. The idea had never occurred to him, though Goethe had been planning a narrative poem on that subject since 1797. Ultimately, a transfer of material was made and, after extensive researches into Swiss history—Schiller never visited Switzerland—composition of the drama was begun on August 25, 1803. Interrupted only by the visit of the talkative Mme. de Staël, the play was completed on February 18, 1804, and the overwhelmingly successful premiere was given at the Weimar Theater on March 17, 1804.

William Tell (*Wilhelm Tell*) was to be Schiller's last complete play. Its 3,291 lines comprise his shortest text, save for the deliberately shorter *Bride of Messina*, which was in a different idiom altogether. By all odds it is his most popular play. For more than a hundred years it drew audiences as no other drama, domestic or foreign, could do. As its centenary approached in 1903, stage statistics show that it was averaging 232 performances a year, while popular repertory pieces reached barely half that number and plays by Lessing and Goethe had less than ten revivals annually. In various translations it became widely known abroad until Tell's apple-shot was integrated into the folklore of Western civilization and until people who did not even know the name of Schiller still knew the gist of *William Tell*. Quite possibly it is the longest-running play in dramatic history.

History and Pseudohistory

As folklore the story began, and folklore it remains, though enthusiasts have sometimes gone so far as to forge historical documents to *make* it true. Long before Schiller, Tell sites had been "established" and the episodes of the legend dated to specific days of the three-week period from October 28 to November 20 (or 21) of the year 1307. The apple-shot is assigned to November 18 (or 19). Yet contemporary historians mention no such matter, nor do church records list any person named William Tell until after 1400. Austrian records mention no uprising of the Swiss cantons in or around the year 1307, nor do they list any governor named Gessler or the assassination of any Austrian bailiff. As far as is known, only native Swiss occupied magistracies in the three cantons in that period. The story appears, full-blown, after 1400, in the *Tell Song* and in *The White Book of Sarnen*, though Schiller's primary source was the *Chronicon Helveticum* of the sixteenth-century historian Aegidius Tschudi (1505–72). This patriotic writer freely admitted that he accepted popular traditions without verification in order to "enhance the honor of the [Swiss] Confederation and of every canton in particular," his opinion being that worthy tales would "cause no harm whatsoever."

Famous shots by famous archers are, moreo common enough in folklore. About 1200 the Da historian Saxo Grammaticus records a similar st about a soldier named Toko. Jealous companions ported to King Harold Bluetooth how Toko boasted he could hit with his arrow a tiny apple set as a distant target, and King Harold maliciou ordered Toko to shoot the apple off the head of own son, with death as the penalty for missing. T made good his boast, but before taking aim he selec three arrows from his quiver. When the king qu tioned him about this, he declared that the other t arrows were for the tyrannical king if he miss After further adventures Toko returned to slay tyrant from ambush. A plausible hypothesis would plain Tell and Toko as Swiss-Alemannic and Scan navian variants, respectively, of a lost, common G manic original hero of legend.

Dramaturgy

In its dramatic technique *William Tell* is a pionee ing work of the first importance, uncannily anticipa ing the motion pictures by a century and total abandoning the traditional world of French classicis

In dramatic time it follows the three-week chrono ogy of the legend, but without insisting on any date Schiller did not even seek to compress time as he d in, say, *Wallenstein*.

In the matter of dramatic place, the scenes are s variously in each of the three "forest cantons" of Ui Schwyz, and Unterwalden, which comprised the ori inal Switzerland. These are grouped around the irregu larly shaped Lake of Lucerne, but Lucerne itself only incidentally connected with the story. A glanc

are spun by many characters, but all strands lead to one nexus: the plight of the Swiss people under their tyrant governor. Tell is merely one among many of the oppressed, until in III, 3, he is forced by the tyrant to shoot the apple off his young son's head. Through Act IV attention centers necessarily on him: his arrest, his escape, his calm assassination of the tyrant from ambush, but once the "deliverance" has been accomplished, Tell recedes into the mass of the population, because the true hero of this play is the Swiss people as a whole.

Characters

In a work so conceived, the characters are primarily components of the total population, representatives of human types and representatives of the various social levels. Among the seven named personages from the canton Uri, for instance, there is a herdsman, a huntsman, and a fisherman, who represent the occupations of the land. Named or unnamed in the cast, there is also a gamekeeper, a sexton, and a priest. This last is hardly distinguishable from a rural Protestant pastor; he lives close to his parishoners and at fitting moments he is on hand to remind them of God's will and God's law. There are also women and children and "many countrymen from the Forest Cantons."

Higher in the social scale are the first-listed in each of the groups of seven of cantonal representatives. Lord Werner Stauffacher of the canton Schwyz is a venerable figure, distressed at his own and the general sufferings, but slow to rebellion. His wife, the Lady Gertrud, is "noble Iberg's daughter," as in Shakespeare's *Julius Caesar* (II, 1) Portia, Brutus's wife, was "a woman well-reputed, Cato's daughter." Both women draw out their husbands' secret thoughts, but in this play of happy outcome, Gertrud, unlike Portia, has already reached the same conclusions as her husband and she urges rebellion; and unlike Portia, who died "by strange manner," she lives to see the rebellion's success. Venerable, too, is Lord Walter Fürst, Tell's father-in-law from the canton Uri. Young Arnold of Melchtal from the canton Unterwalden, on the other hand, stands in lieu of his own venerable father, who has been tortured and blinded at the tyrant's instigation. It is young Arnold's frantic grief that prods Stauffacher and Fürst into action, and from the conference of the three of them emerges the much larger conference on the Rütli meadow, that historical event that led to Swiss independence.

Higher still in rank is the aged Baron von Attinghausen, whose declining years are darkened by the alienation of his nephew and heir, Ulrich von Rudenz. This good-hearted youth is so infatuated with the glamor of Austrian court life that he scorns the "peasant aristocracy" of his native land and is bored by the simple life among these mountain valleys. The argument between uncle and nephew in II, 1 echoes a bitterer argument in Shakespeare's *Richard II* (II, 1) between the aged John of Gaunt and his brash young nephew, King Richard. Once again, the overall happy outcome of the present play requires both a conciliatory Attinghausen and a Rudenz won over, if belatedly, to the right cause. The same scene from *Richard II* also gives the cue for IV, 2, where the dying Attinghausen, like the dying John of Gaunt, eulogizes his country and foretells its future:

"The nobles come down from their ancient castles
And swear their civic oaths unto the cities.

.   .   .

I see the Princes and the noble lords
Approaching in their armor to make war
Against an inoffensive folk of herdsmen.
The struggle will be unto death, and many
A pass will be made glorious by bloody
Decision. With bare breast the peasant will
Fall a free martyr in the host of lances,
But he will break them, and the flower of nobles
Will fall, and freedom lift victorious banners.
Therefore stand firm together—inseparable—
Let no free place be alien to another—
Set beacon fires a-top your mountains so
That league with league may swiftly be assembled—
Be one— Be one— Be one— "

The courtly aspirations of young Rudenz are largely the result of his love for the pretty noblewoman, Berta of Bruneck, but during a tryst by a mountain waterfall (III, 2), in the course of a hunting party, she rebukes him sharply and bids him stand with his own people and country. The two of them, plus Attinghausen, stand in this play as representatives of the noble class, for in Schiller's "dramatic shorthand" all classes of society share in Switzerland's liberation and glorious future. But here the dramatic shorthand fails to work properly. The love tryst is coy, the winning over of Rudenz is so rapid as to make him seem feather-witted, and Berta is so wholesome as to be unbelievable. Against the sinister tyranny and general suffering, the whole episode appears frivolous. We note here a last vestige of aristocratic taste, as the only love affair in the play is assigned to youthful and leisured nobles. Thus, the roles of Rudenz and Berta have proved to be ungrateful ones—a rare case of audience objection to a love interest in a serious play.

The Title Role

Probably nowhere in drama is there a title role with so few lines as the role of Tell. The play opens as an Alpine idyll, all sunlight and melodious cowbells and simple countrymen talking about their herds. Then a muffled roar is heard from the mountains, signaling an oncoming storm. The lake is seen roughening with wind and waves. In rushes Konrad Baumgarten: a burgrave of the emperor's tried to violate Baumgarten's wife and he split the man's skull with an ax. Pursuers are close on his trail and he must get across the lake. Impossible, says the ferryman, until the storm is past. At line 127, Tell appears. He speaks only seventeen lines before he takes the fugitive into a boat and starts to row him to the further shore. The 182-line scene ends with the arrival of the thwarted posse.

Act I, Scene 2 presents the grave discussion between Lord Werner Stauffacher and the Lady Gertrud. As they withdraw, Tell enters with Baumgarten, to whom he speaks four lines, bidding him go to Stauffacher for help.

In I, 3, in the public square near Altorf, we witness the forced labor at the new Fortress Keep of Uri, and we see the establishment of the absurd hat on a pole, symbol of authority, before which all passers-by must genuflect. Along comes Tell in conversation with Stauffacher, to whom he speaks a total of twenty-six lines, concluding with the rhymed quatrain:

> "Do as you will, but spare me your transactions.
> I am not one to ponder and to choose;
> If you want me for some specific actions,
> Then call on Tell, and I am yours to use."

The fourth scene brings together the three cantonal representatives, Fürst, Stauffacher, and young Melchtal, and the distraught Melchtal reports the bailiff's torture of his father. Plans are made for a larger gathering on the Rütli meadow. Tell does not appear at all. So ends the 751-line Act I, in which the hero has spoken forty-seven lines and appeared in three scenes out of four.

In Act II he does not appear at all. Of two scenes, the first consists of the uncle-nephew colloquy in Attinghausen's baronial hall, while the long II, 2 presents the famous nocturnal assembly on the Rütli meadow where countrymen swear an oath to resist the foreign tyranny.

Act III, Scene 1 is a brief scene in Tell's dooryard, depicting the hero at home with his wife and two small sons. The Rudenz-Berta tryst occupies III, 2. But with III, 3 we come to the famous scene of the apple-shot.

Before the foolish hat-on-the-pole, two guards, Hardheart and Folklove, are complaining, as the scene opens, about how only riffraff do homage to this symbol of authority, while decent people make detours to avoid doing so. Tell comes walking along in talk with his small son Walter and fails to genuflect. Hardheart arrests him as little Walter sets up a clamor. A crowd gathers, the altercation grows, and at its height Bailiff Gessler enters on horseback, his falcon on his wrist, and accompanied by a large retinue, "who form a ring of pikes around the entire stage." The tyrant refuses to be satisfied with Tell's apology and bids him shoot an apple off Walter's head at eighty paces, twenty less than the boast he has heard reported of the archer. With great skill, Schiller builds up the tension and excitement. Tell pleads for alternatives, Gessler is adamant, the boy is fearless. Tell selects a second arrow, which he sticks into his doublet. Berta and Rudenz, who are of Gessler's hunting party, vehemently intervene, and Rudenz challenges Gessler with his sword. Amid the confusion the arrow is sped, the apple is shot through the center, and Walter runs triumphantly back to his father. Gessler then inquires about that second arrow, and when Tell explains that it was for him in case the boy was killed, the tyrant has Tell led away in fetters and the crowd is left in consternation.

Act IV opens on the further lakeshore amid a storm. A fisherman and his son are watching a boat in peril amid the gusting wind and billowing waves. The fisher lad recognizes it as the bailiff's boat, and from the previous scene we know Tell is a prisoner on board. A bell is ringing through the wind and rain to sound the alarm for the boat. The watchers announce that the boat is close inshore just beyond a spur of cliffs. All of a sudden there is Tell, alive and free, on land. In an uncharacteristically long speech, he describes the pilot's despair and Gessler's terror and how they unchained him as the only man who might steer the boat to safety; he took the helm, steered close in, and in a daring maneuver swung the craft about, jumped to the cliff, and kicked the boat back out to the deep waters. The fisherman and his son will report the escape to Tell's wife and friends, but Tell himself sets out for an unnamed destination.

Act IV, Scene 2 contains the prophecy of the dying Attinghausen, the full and enthusiastic conversion of Rudenz to the right cause, and the plans for immediate and concerted action against the oppressor.

With IV, 3 we come to the climactic scene of Gessler's slaying. The theater audience is looking up the slope of the Sunken Road near Küssnacht, a short but narrow passage between tree-overgrown rocks, which Schiller magnifies into cliffs. With crossbow in hand, Tell comes and stations himself at the foot of the slope and there speaks a ninety-one-line soliloquy. Why he should speak at such length is a puzzle. The first eight lines would suffice to announce that he is here to intercept and kill Gessler; the rest are commonplace thoughts, revealing nothing we do not know already; it does not even portray a moral struggle. If it is a device for suspense, there are one hundred thirty-five further lines that more effectively build up suspense until the moment when the arrow pierces Gessler's heart. A wedding party passes up the Sunken Road and Tell exchanges comments about it with the gamekeeper. A woman named Armgard plants herself and her children at the foot of the road in order to halt Gessler and plead to him for her imprisoned husband. Tell meanwhile has withdrawn to a position of ambush. At last Gessler appears on horseback with a mounted companion. Armgard's plea is being roughly denied when Tell's arrow speeds to its target. After a small crowd has gathered and dispersed, some Brothers of Mercy are singing a dirge over the corpse as the curtain falls.

The Tell legend consisted of only two scenes, the apple-shot and the slaying of Gessler, plus the report of the hero's escape from the boat, and it is noteworthy that Schiller exploited these elements to the full but did not seek to expand them unduly or to eke out a five-act play with new adventures for the hero.

Act V, Scene 1 is the joyous festival of a liberated people. The grim Fortress Keep of Uri, which we saw in I, 3 under construction with forced labor, is now being torn to pieces, its beams and scaffolding being thrown down with crash and thud as we watch. An immensely effective stage business, this, and audiences experience almost a kinetic excitement in that gleeful destruction. People from afar are summoned by the Alpine horn, whose blower is called the Bull of Uri. Crowds gather and gather, but Tell is absent.

By rights, this scene should pass directly to the ten-line final scene, and in most performances that is precisely what is done. Schiller, however, intruded the tolerably long V, 2, set inside Tell's house, where a fugitive monk is seeking refuge. The monk proves to be John the Parricide (Johannes Parracida), an Austrian duke who has slain his uncle, the emperor, to avenge a personal wrong. With aversion Tell bids him journey on to Rome and make his confession to the pope.

Then, to make a scene-change, the wall of Tell's cottage is drawn aside, and the jubilant throng arrives in the yard to salute the hero and national liberator.

The Nature of the Play

William Tell was Schiller's third consecutive play with a medieval setting, and we have seen how he understood the Middle Ages as an era when anything might happen, as an era of legends and wonders. Like *The Maid of Orleans* and like *The Bride of Messina*, this play is essentially, we believe, a legend. Schiller had lived through the American Revolution (age seventeen to age twenty-four) and through the French Revolution (age thirty to age thirty-six). Despite his honorary citizenship in the French First Republic, he was appalled by the course of revolution in France. Had he wished to create a dramatic paradigm of revolution, he could surely have chosen a subject other than the Tell legend. The tyrant's overthrow portrayed in this play was a fiction, as Schiller knew, and it took place allegedly five hundred years ago as the spontaneous action of a uniformly good people under the auspices of God. Nowhere is there a tumbril or a guillotine or a Fouquier-Tinville or a Robespierre. In fact, nobody gets killed except Gessler. It reflects neither of the revolutions of Schiller's lifetime, and as a blueprint for future revolutions it is pitifully inadequate.

It is, rather, a gentle tale of happy outcome about a folk hero of long ago. Its literary analogues are to be found among the labors of Heracles. In many respects it may also be fairly described as a Rousseauistic idyll for the stage. Its setting is Jean-Jacques's own Switzerland, with its wholesome people uncorrupted by courts and cities, and dwelling, in nature's intended way, close to both earth and sky. The notion of Switzerland as a second Eden, moreover, was not Rousseau's alone. As long ago as 1728, Albrecht von Haller made his Swiss journey and committed his reverent enthusiasms to verse in the long-admired poem, *The Alps*, which, incidentally was organized into "scenes" of narrative. Thus, *William Tell* stands as the culmination of seventy-five years of a literary and a popular tradition about Switzerland and its simple and good people.

Legend and idyll it was and is, but it was also a spectacle play containing "something for everyone." Those twelve outdoor sets affording "views of Switzerland" were alone worth the price of admission. Bailiff Gessler's two entrances on horseback were immensely arresting, and in both his scenes there was the thrilling optical illusion of flying arrows where no arrows actually flew. These were elements of the circus, just as many a passage in the plays embody elements of the opera. And then there were the novel sound effects: the songs, the storms, the signal bell, the Alpine horn blown by the Bull of Uri, the destruction noises of the Fortress Keep of Uri as it was torn apart. Only the offstage hunting horns during the Rudenz-Berta tryst were familiar.

In 1804 all this was stunningly new. And for a hundred years, audiences found *William Tell* a glorious entertainment. It was a jolly yet noble show that sent everyone home in good humor, children and oldsters alike delighted in it, and its charm seemed inexhaustible.

In the Twentieth Century

In the twentieth century the play has fared otherwise. In 1913, the year before World War I started, Gerhardt Hauptmann staged a realistic *William Tell* in muted tones, with the Swiss as clumsy peasants, but still with elaborate stage sets. In 1919, the year following the war, Leopold Jessner's production withdrew the story from Switzerland altogether and put his players on platforms and steps. Black backdrops gaped near their tops to afford glimpses of mountain peaks and sky, symbols of freedom. This production drew protests from the political right.

Since 1950 the play has been pulled and hauled by both the left and the right to make propaganda for revolution and for the political aims of both Germanies. Then, in the 1966 production in Wiesbaden, the direction by Hansgünther Heyme made the work over completely.

Not the regular theater curtain, but the iron fire curtain confronted the audience assembling. The iron fire curtain rose to reveal an irregularly shaped platform approached by steps and lighted by garish reflectors; the curtain remained up until the end of the performance. Cowbells, songs, and herdsmen were omitted. Out staggered a bloodstained Baumgarten clad in primitive hides and begging for rescue. The surly ferryman did not reply, merely thumbed toward the oncoming storm, but a hulking brute of a Tell came along and undertook the rowing of the boat because it displayed his strength.

In the second scene the Stauffachers squatted on stools, apart and estranged. He, in steel-rimmed glasses, bald, stultified with wealth, let himself be inveigled by her into trying his hand at politics. In the third scene, proletarian workers hauled a huge stone in a net up the platform steps—building the Fortress Keep of Uri—but dropped their burden as the noon whistle blew.

Melchtal was a bully. Attinghausen was a superannuated officer unsteadily bracing on his rusty dress sword. Rudenz was a grinning oaf in a tomato-red hunting jacket. Berta was a sly slut who won Rudenz over to the good cause by frank bosom-and-thigh-displays; she even fingered his fly. The oath-swearing on the Rütli was a Nazi brawl, with Stauffacher now still more closely resembling Dr. Goebbels and with the oath formula half-chanted to a variant of the "Horst Wessel Song." In the apple-shot scene, Gessler was a weary tyrant and Tell swaggered over his shooting skill. At home Tell browbeat his cowed wife and knocked his boys about with a hefty hand. In the assassination scene, Gessler appeared drenched to the skin and bedraggled, the bridal pair were tottering oldsters, and the Brothers of Mercy sang their dirge in falsetto. The final scene was a near-ballet of club-wielding brutes singing the variant of the "Horst Wessel Song."

Clearly this production was a work of sheer hate. Not even the superwholesome *William Tell* merited this kind of defamation.

AN AFTERWORD

Demetrius would have been Schiller's eighth historical play; significantly, it deals with the history of still another country. Its subject was the meteoric rise and fall of the young Russian who led a Polish army into his homeland to overthrow the usurper Boris Godunov. The two acts nearly completed before his death show Schiller's dramatic and poetic powers at their height.

To Schiller, European history was the proper "quarry" for dramatic materials, but not for patriotic plays, glorifying one nation. The dramatist's aim should be universality. History contained things old enough to allow perspective, yet recent enough to be relevant to his own time. The task of the dramatic poet was then to order the free-ranging characters into configurations from which the thoughtful spectator could infer the durable principles of human life.

What mattered to Schiller was human beings, whom he believed to be the same at all times and in all places; "accidentals" changed, but the moral truth behind the "accidentals" was changeless. He felt that the dramatist had a duty to reveal moral truth, but he also felt that access to moral truth lay within the realm of art.

Schiller's theme was mankind. The objective of his art was timelessness, and he deemed art a sacred thing and apart. Out of these convictions rises the sense of exaltation that his dramas convey.

BIBLIOGRAPHY

Works by Schiller

Die Räuber. Frankfurt-am-Main/Leipzig, 1781.
Die Verschwörung des Fiesko zu Genua. Mannheim, 1783.
Kabale und Liebe. Mannheim, 1784. —*Intrigue and Love*. Translated by Charles E. Passage. New York, 1971.
Don Carlos, Infant von Spanien. Leipzig, 1787. —*Don Carlos, Infante of Spain*. Translated by Charles E. Passage. New York, 1959.
Wallenstein. 2 vols. Tübingen, 1800. —*Wallenstein: A Historical Drama in Three Parts*. Translated by Charles E. Passage. New York, 1960.
Die Jungfrau von Orleans. In *Kalender auf das Jahr 1802*. Berlin, 1801. —*The Maid of Orleans*. In *Mary Stuart; The Maid of Orleans*. Translated by Charles E. Passage. New York, 1961.
Maria Stuart. Tübingen, 1801. —*Mary Stuart*. In *Mary Stuart; The Maid of Orleans*. Translated by Charles E. Passage. New York, 1961.
Die Braut von Messina, oder Die feindlichen Brüder. Tübingen, 1803. —*The Bride of Messina*. In *The Bride of Messina; William Tell; Demetrius*. Translated by Charles E. Passage. New York, 1962.

195

Wilhelm Tell. Tübingen, 1804. —*William Tell.* In *The Bride of Messina; William Tell; Demetrius.* Translated by Charles E. Passage. New York, 1962.

Demetrius. Fragment. Edited by C. G. Körner. In *Morgenblatt* (Tübingen/Stuttgart), Nos. 258–59, 281 (1815). —*Demetrius.* In *The Bride of Messina; William Tell; Demetrius.* Translated by Charles E. Passage. New York, 1962.

2. ESSAYS, STORIES, HISTORICAL WRITINGS

Geschichte des Abfalls der vereinigten Niederlande von der spanischen Regierung. 2 vols. Leipzig, 1788.

Der Geisterseher. A novel fragment. Leipzig, 1789.

Geschichte des dreyßigjährigen Kriegs. 3 vols. Leipzig, 1791–93.

Über den Grund des Vergnügens an tragischen Gegenständen. 1792.

Verbrecher aus verlorener Ehre. In *Kleinere prosaische Schriften.* 4 vols. 1792–1802. Originally published as *Verbrecher aus Infamie.* In *Thalia* (Leipzig), 2, No. 1 (1786).

Über Anmuth und Würde. Leipzig, 1793.

Über die ästhetische Erziehung des Menschen. In *Die Horen* (Tübingen), Nos. 1, 2, 6 (1795). —*On the Aesthetic Education of Man.* Translated by Reginald Snell. London, 1954.

Über naive und sentimentalische Dichtung. In *Die Horen* (Tübingen), Nos. 11–12 (1795), No. 1 (1796). —*Naïve and Sentimental Poetry.* In *Naïve and Sentimental Poetry; On the Sublime.* Translated by Julius A. Elias. New York, 1966.

3. COLLECTED EDITIONS IN GERMAN

Kleinere prosaische Schriften. 4 vols. 1792–1802.

Gedichte. 2 vols. 1800–1803.

Sämtliche Werke. Edited by C. G. Körner. 12 vols. 1812–15.

Briefe. Edited by F. Jonas. 7 vols. 1892–96.

Briefwechsel mit W. von Humboldt. Edited by A. Leitzmann. 1900.

Sämtliche Werke. Edited by E. von der Hellen. 16 vols. 1904f.

Sämtliche Werke. Edited by C. Schüddekopf and C. Jöfer. 22 vols. 1910–26.

Gespräche. Edited by J. Petersen. 1911.

Briefwechsel zwischen Schiller und Goethe. Edited by G. Gräf and A. Leitzmann. 3 vols. 1912. New edition, 1955.

4. COLLECTED EDITIONS IN
ENGLISH TRANSLATION

Friedrich Schiller: An Anthology for Our Time. Bilingual edition. Edited by Frederick Ungar. 1959.

Works about Schiller

Buchwald, R. *Schiller: Leben und Werk.* Wiesbaden, 1959.

Carlyle, Thomas. *Life of Schiller.* London, 1825.

Elias, Julius A. Introduction to *Naive and Sentimental Poetry,* by Friedrich Schiller. New York, 1966.

Emrich, Wilhelm. "Schiller and the Antinomies of Human Society." In *The Literary Revolution and Modern Society.* New York, 1971.

Heller, Erich. "In Two Minds about Schiller." In *The Artist's Journey into the Interior.* New York, 1968.

Kühnemann, Eugen. *Schiller.* Munich, 1908.

Mann, Thomas. *Versuch über Schiller.* Berlin, 1955.

———. "On Schiller." In *Last Essays.* New York, 1959.

Seidlin, Oskar. "Schiller: Poet of Politics." In *A Schiller Symposium,* edited by Leslie A. Willson. Austin, Texas, 1961.

Snell, Reginald. Introduction to *On the Aesthetic Education of Man,* by Friedrich Schiller. London, 1954.

Spender, Stephen. "Schiller, Shakespeare and the Theme of

Power." In *A Schiller Symposium*, edited by Leslie A. Willson. Austin, Texas, 1961.

Storz, Gerhardt. *Das Drama Friedrich Schillers.* 1938.

Ungar, Frederick. "An Account of Schiller's Life and Work." In *Friedrich Schiller: An Anthology for Our Time*, edited by Frederick Ungar. New York, 1959.

Weigand, Hermann J. "Schiller: Transfiguration of a Titan." In *A Schiller Symposium*, edited by Leslie A. Willson. Austin, Texas, 1961.

————. "Illustrations to Highlight Some Points in Schiller's Essay on Poetry." In *Surveys and Soundings in European Literature*. Princeton, N.J., 1966.

Wiese, Benno von. *Friedrich Schiller.* Stuttgart, 1959.

INDEX